God Dreams

How to hear God's voice in dreams and visions

Tania Harris, PhD

Copyright © 2024 Tania Harris

30 29 28 27 26 25 24   7 6 5 4 3 2 1

First published 2024 by Authentic Media Limited,
PO Box 6326, Bletchley, Milton Keynes, MK1 9GG.
authenticmedia.co.uk

The right of Tania Harris to be identified as the Author of this Work
has been asserted in accordance with the
Copyright, Designs and Patents Act 1988.

All rights reserved.
No part of this publication may be reproduced, stored
in a retrieval system, or transmitted in any form or by any means,
electronic, mechanical, photocopying, recording or otherwise, without
the prior permission of the publisher or a licence permitting restricted
copying. In the UK such licences are issued by the Copyright Licensing
Agency, 5th Floor, Shackleton House, 4 Battle Bridge Lane, London SE1 2HX.

British Library Cataloguing in Publication Data
A catalogue record for this book is available from the British Library.
ISBN: 978-1-78893-395-7
978-1-78893-396-4 (e-book)

Scripture quotations taken from
The Holy Bible, New International Version Anglicised
Copyright © 1979, 1984, 2011 Biblica
Used by permission of Hodder & Stoughton Ltd, an Hachette UK company.
All rights reserved.
'NIV' is a registered trademark of Biblica
UK trademark number 1448790.

Illustrations by S4Carlisle Publishing Services.

Cover design by Rick Carter, studiooneanother.com.au
Printed and bound by CPI Group (UK) Ltd, Croydon, CR0 4YY

'As a psychotherapist, I've experienced the delight that comes with accompanying people on a deeper walk with God. For me, the psychological and the spiritual have always been deeply entwined. Tania's book *God Dreams* reflects this perspective and works to integrate them in a fresh and practical way. God does indeed speak to us in imagery and dreams, often from outside our conscious awareness. Learning to listen to these "messages from beyond" helps us to process our daily walk in the world and make concrete what God has for us. I'm thrilled to recommend Tania's very articulate and profound approach to deepening our sense of God and how we can share more fully in the promises he has for us!'

Dinah Eades Buchanan (M. Couns. Grad Dip Gestalt; Grad Dip Spiritual Direction), Clinical Supervisor, Psychotherapist, Spiritual Director and Educator

'Rev Dr. Harris's groundbreaking work, *God Dreams*, adds a much-needed synthesis to the growing conversation on lived spirituality. In a day and age when many are deconstructing their faith, Harris offers a biblically and theologically sound meditation on these widely misunderstood phenomena to create a bridge between faith and empiricism. But, more importantly, Harris's work is practical, full of examples and instructive suggestions. Refusing the typical Charismatic reductionism that turns complex experiences into neat packages, Harris sensitively qualifies, describes and explores the many dimensions of dreams and visions from biblical times to the contemporary moment. Refreshingly ecumenical and scholarly sourced with a conversational and accessible style, *God Dreams* sets a new standard for pastoral and lay resources on dreams and visions.'

Benjamin Crace PhD, Professor of Religious Studies, Tennessee Technological University

'Rev Dr. Tania Harris has done a truly thorough work in laying out the spiritual, neurological and practical elements of dreaming in this book. By pulling each dimension together like drawstrings into the centre of God's wisdom, we discover some of the wondrous ways that the Holy Spirit communicates to us and in us all. Tania's detailed explanation of dream-life is written in a conversational style that is rich with revelation and contemporary examples, making it a most enjoyable read. This book will awaken in readers a fresh desire to pay close attention to their dreams and follow the relational course set by Jesus. Dream-visions are finally being recognized as a place where heavenly realities are unearthed and the Spirit counsels us in our innermost person. Readers, the night is still young! I recommend reading this before sleeping!'

Isi de Gersigny, Senior Pastor, Jubilee Church;
Leader, Australian Prophetic Council, Australia

'This is a brilliant book on a vital subject for anyone serious about hearing (and seeing) the word of God today. Dreams and visions are, according to Scripture, one of the primary ways in which God wishes to communicate with us, but they are particularly open to misunderstanding, negligence and downright abuse. Tania Harris does a great job combining her academic rigour and love for the Scriptures with personal experience in a way that will equip many to experience God's leading in exciting and life-changing ways. The church needs this book!'

Pete Greig, Founder, 24-7 Prayer International, and author of
How to Hear God: A Simple Guide for Normal People

'Imagine missing the voice of God! Tania cares so much for the church that she has written a book to ensure it doesn't happen. While advocating for God's voice in the words of Scripture, she presents the case that God still speaks through dreams and visions outside Scripture. Her analysis of the visionary experiences of Peter the apostle and John in Revelation provides insights into discernment, discipleship and the power of the Holy Spirit. Whether you spend your time behind the pulpit or in the pew, this book will convince you that we all need to "wake up" to the reality of God's voice as we sleep. *God Dreams* is written in an easy-to-read style that will cause you to stop and think as you uncover its many important truths. Everyone should read this book!'

Revd Paul Hudson, General Secretary,
Elim Churches Global

'Everyone dreams, but it takes a prophetic specialist like Tania Harris to awaken us to the possibility that God might be speaking through them! Drawing on psychology, neuroscience, Scripture and experience, Harris takes her readers on a fascinating (and perhaps life-changing) journey into a realm we need to stop ignoring. The book is packed with intriguing personal stories and some provocative insights into the Bible. Don't ignore it!'

Revd Dr Jon Newton, Associate Professor and Revelation Scholar,
Alphacrucis College, Australia

'Dreams never cease to amaze me with their clever details and layered messaging. God designs these "night visions" like a book with chapters, themes and characters, so that careful and thoughtful detective work is often needed to investigate them! Tania Harris's book *God Dreams* provides the training we need to sort through the puzzle pieces and identify God's voice in them. With her pastoral and scholarly background, the book provides a thorough explanation of the language of dreams and visions and reflects her deep care for the church. I am blessed to endorse this well-written book that will help build a prophetic culture in every local church. *God Dreams* is brilliant and will help many. A must-read!'

Maria Mason, Senior Leader, Tribe Church;
Member, Australian Prophetic Council, Australia

'You only have to spend a few minutes on social media to see all the misunderstandings surrounding dreams and visions. It's no wonder that so many prefer to politely ignore them. But in *God Dreams*, Tania skilfully, practically, historically and academically cuts a clear path through the jungle of noise. She directs us back to the Bible, gives us simple, profound truths about God's visual forms of communication and backs it up with real-life stories of ordinary people. Readers will find their lives enriched as they explore this fresh aspect of their relationship with God.'

David Shadbolt, Co-founder and Coaching Lead,
School of Prophecy, UK

To Pete,
who not only listened to my dreams but helped carry them to fulfilment

Contents

Thank You		xi
Author's Note		xiii

Part I The Nature of Dreams and Visions — **1**

1	The First Time I Had a God-Dream	3
2	What Are Dreams and Visions?	12
3	The Language of Dream-Visions	31
4	When a Dream Is Not a Dream	48
5	Where Do Dreams Come From?	61

Part II How to Understand Your Dream-Visions — **83**

6	Anatomy of a Dream	85
7	Peter's Vision of an Unappetizing Lunch	96
8	Your Customized Dream Dictionary	107
9	The ABCs of Symbols	121
10	John's Vision of the Heavenly Government	136
11	More on Symbols (1): The Dragon and a Pregnant Woman	152
12	More on Symbols (2): Two Kingdoms at War	161
13	How Do You Know It's a God-Dream?	174
14	After We Wake Up	185
15	Meeting God in a Dream	196

| 16 | Awakening Your Dreams | 207 |

Notes 218
Bibliography 230

Thank You

Like many books, this one was years in the making. It began with the first God-dream I experienced as a young adult and has continued to the point where the most common way I hear God today is when I sleep! Though hearing God in dreams has become more familiar through the years, I still find myself surprised. Surprised that God could speak like this, surprised at the biblical record and then surprised by how many in the church don't relate. To this day, the cleverness and artistry of God's visual communiqués keeps me in awe.

It saddens me that many in the Western Church have not embraced God's favoured form of communication, though I understand their reasons. My prayer is that this book will be part of the solution.

Heartfelt thanks must go to my ever-patient covenant brothers and sisters who have acted as conversation partners in the journey. Dream-vision interpretation is not a solo activity and I couldn't have done it without them. Anita, Pete, Claire and Vicki – thank you for your listening ears as we've reflected on our God-dreams and then your faithful and open hearts as we've journeyed together to see them outworked.

Another thank-you must also go to my beta-readers who painstakingly read the manuscript, picked up errors and gave feedback. Thank you to Anita Pahor, Paul Hudson, Ben Crace, Vicki Clarke, Martyn Webb, Pernille Liland, Dinah Buchanan, John and Beth Allison, Nikki Dent, Jon Newton, Tony Cooke, David Shadbolt and Michelle Felice. You've made this book better with every word.

Thank you too to John Christopher Thomas and the Revelation Scholars group that allowed me to join for a year while I worked through the chapters on John's visions in Revelation. It was an honour to glean from your scholarship and wisdom.

Finally, thank you to those who have given me permission to tell your stories. What a privilege to marvel together at the power and beauty of the Holy Spirit shining through each one! I pray they will bless many.

Author's Note

Throughout the book, I frequently use the male pronouns 'he', 'his' and 'him' to refer to God. This is a not due to a conviction that God is male, but rather a reflection of the limitations of the English language and the absence of a gender-neutral personal pronoun (i.e. God should not be called 'it'). The Scriptures are clear that the Creator God is Spirit, and as such is neither male nor female. In God, both males and females find their identity (Gen. 1:26–27; John 4:24).

In my reference to the Holy Spirit, at times, I choose to apply the definite article 'the' to denote the Spirit, and at other times, I omit it. This is intentional, as it acknowledges that Holy Spirit is a person and therefore grammatically requires no definite article.

PART I

THE NATURE OF DREAMS AND VISIONS

The First Time I Had a God-Dream

A Thief in the Night

The first time I had a God-dream was in the middle of a difficult season in my life. It was one of those moments when God seemed agonizingly, run-your-fingernails-down-the-chalkboard *slow*. Frustration had risen to boiling point and threatened to erupt in a volcanic display. Why was God so slow?! When was he going to do what he promised?

My solution was an attempt to project-manage God. I even had timelines and subtasks: 'God, if you could do this *now*, then I could do *this* . . . Or, if you did this *next month*, then I could do *that* . . .'

Then I had a dream. In the dream, I woke up to discover my apartment had been broken into. Items of jewellery, cash from my handbag, and my stereo had all been stolen.

My first instinct was to check the time, so I looked to the clock on my bedside table. Oddly, the clock hands were spinning round and round and I couldn't read the display.

It's okay, I thought, *I have a digital clock on the other side of the room*. But when I looked at the digital clock, its digits were all scrambled and I couldn't read them.

What time is it?! I cried out. *And who has sabotaged my clocks?!*

My next thought was: *How could a thief have broken into my house while I was sleeping? Surely I would have woken up?*

Then I literally woke up.

Afterwards, the feelings from the dream lingered as I showered and dressed for the day. I felt frustrated and powerless – even stupid: why didn't I wake up? Surely the noise of a thief breaking into my flat would have woken me?

But it was *just a dream*, so I shrugged it off and turned to my morning coffee and quiet time.

At the time, I had been using a devotional book with daily Bible readings. The reading for that day was from Matthew chapter 24: 'If the owner of the house had known at what time of night the thief was coming, he would have kept watch and would not have let his house be broken into. So you also must be ready, because the Son of Man will come at an hour when you do not expect him' (vv. 43–44).

What?

Suddenly my dream didn't feel so ethereal any more.

That day was a Tuesday – and I was working at a local Bible college. With visions of clocks, oversleeping and thieves fresh in my mind, I drove to work, greeted my colleagues and headed to the downstairs classroom for our weekly staff meeting.

After the usual briefing and announcements, the principal began to share an exhortation from the Scriptures: 'Turn your Bibles to Matthew chapter 25.'

My Bible fell open easily.

The principal then began talking about one of Jesus' well-known parables. In the story, ten bridesmaids were waiting for a wedding. Their role was to prepare the bride for the groom's arrival, which in Jewish custom was typically at night. Five of them were deemed foolish because they didn't have enough oil in their lamps and they blew out. The other five were wise because they had plenty of oil to keep them burning. When the groom was delayed and they all fell asleep, only the wise bridesmaids were ready when the groom eventually arrived. The foolish, on the other hand, were not ready and were shut out of the wedding.

On finishing his retelling of the story, the principal paused and scanned the room: 'Some of you here are like those five foolish bridesmaids – you've been waiting for the promises of God, but it's been too long and you've fallen asleep. God is telling you to keep oil in your lamp and stay awake! Even though you don't know what time it is, be ready! Trust God for the timing and stay faithful to what he's said.'

While They Were Sleeping

We know that God speaks in a variety of ways, but in church life we are particularly familiar with two. The first is via the

Scriptures – when we're reading the Bible and the Spirit takes a principle from the text and applies it to our situation. It's almost as if the verses 'jump off the page' and land directly in our hearts.

The second way is through preaching – when we're listening to a sermon and our hearts begin to quicken as the Spirit nails us with a message we need to hear. It feels as though the preacher is reading our mail.

That morning, God had used both these methods, but he'd also spoken in a dream. At the time, it seemed absurd. Since when did God speak in dreams?

I had never heard anyone talk about it. I'd never heard it in a sermon or read it in a Christian book. When I told my friends about the dream, they shrugged their shoulders. My pastor called me strange.

Then I started rereading my Bible, and I was shocked by what I found.

Biblically speaking, hearing from God in dreams and visions is 'normal'. These colourful and creative experiences communicate in a sort of picture language, and there are hundreds of them in the Bible. One commentator has said that if you were to take all the dreams and visions out of Scripture, you would remove more than one-third of its contents.[1] Another has counted 700 separate visionary experiences.[2] While today we tend to distinguish dreams and visions by our level of consciousness – so we have 'dreams' while we're asleep and 'visions' while we're awake – the terms are used interchangeably in Scripture, and nearly every Bible character experiences them.

The First Time I Had a God-Dream

For a quick snapshot, there's Abraham dreaming of a blazing torch passing through bloody animal parts, the symbols of ancient treaty-making (Gen. 15:1–20), and Jacob seeing angels flying up and down a staircase, initiating a life-changing decision (Gen. 28:10–22). There's Gideon gaining military assurance through a vision of a speeding bread roll (Judg. 7:9–14) and Solomon dreaming of a genie-like offer he can't refuse (1 Kgs 3:5). There's Joseph and Daniel, Jeremiah and Zechariah, as well as unlikely pagans such as Abimelech, the Egyptian pharaoh and the Babylonian king Nebuchadnezzar. Later, there's Amos with his basket of ripe fruit (Amos 8), Zechariah getting a clothing makeover (Zech. 3) and Ezekiel with a vision of spinning celestial wheels (Ezek. 1).

Fast forward to the New Testament and there's Pilate's wife dreaming of Jesus' innocence (Matt. 27:19), the apostle Peter envisaging a menu of unappetizing food while waiting for lunch (Matt. 17:19), and the apostle Paul receiving travel directions while he slept (Acts 16:9). And who could forget John living out a veritable movie of fantastical scenes in his visions of Revelation (Rev. 1:9,17).

When we take a closer look at Scripture, we see that many of the most pivotal points in biblical history began while someone was sleeping!

We Don't Recognize It

The God of the Bible hasn't changed. The Spirit is still communicating in visual forms today. It took a dream about broken clocks and spiritual slumber for me to realize it. God was speaking an important message about his timing in my life that enabled me to walk through the season with grace and patience. I'm glad I noticed it.

My lack of awareness about dreams and visions in the early years of my spiritual journey is true of the contemporary church everywhere – at least in the West. God is speaking by his Spirit in dreams and visions, but we don't always recognize it.[3]

The irony is that many of us struggle to hear from God. It's a refrain I hear across the global church: 'I can't hear God's voice!' We are like the ancients in one of the oldest books of the Bible complaining that God doesn't speak (Job 33:13).

But what is the real problem here? The Scripture goes on to say:

> For God *does* speak – now one way, now another –
>   though *no one perceives it*.
> In a dream, in a vision of the night,
>   when deep sleep falls on people
>   as they slumber in their beds.
>
> *Job 33:14–15, italics mine*

While the author of this verse (Elihu) was not someone who could always be counted on for his theological advice (God later rejected it, Job 42:7), his words reflect the understanding of his day: God *was* speaking – in dreams and visions – but people didn't notice. So the problem was *not* with God's desire or ability to communicate. The problem was with humanity for not perceiving it.

The same is true for us today. The Scriptures show that the Creator God is a communicator – it's in his very nature to speak (Ps. 115:4–7). Divine communication enables us to know God personally and join with him in his plans. In fact, God does nothing *without first revealing it* prophetically (Amos 3:7).[4] Under the Old Covenant, it was largely specially appointed prophets who heard God's voice, but under the New Covenant, all can hear him speak (Acts 2:17). The Spirit speaks today to continue Jesus' mission, reminding us of everything he established (John 14:26) and then applying it to our lives (John 16:13). Jesus himself said that heeding his voice was the essence of discipleship (John 10:27). God speaks, his people respond in faith, and God's plan unfolds. This is the pattern throughout biblical history.

This also explains why Scripture repeatedly admonishes us to hear and respond to God's voice (e.g. Isa. 55:2; Matt. 11:15; Heb. 3:7–8). God *is* speaking, even when we don't notice it. And so the onus falls to us. We must learn to recognize God's voice in dream-visions so that we can follow it. The call echoes through our biblical past and remains with us today: 'Listen and hear my voice; pay attention and hear what I say' (Isa. 28:23).

Aim of the Book

Since my dream about the thief in the night, dreams and visions have become the most common way God speaks to me. The Spirit has spoken about my personal life, my career and my relationships – all in dreams. Some of those experiences have been life-changing; in other cases, the experience has been just one of many small steps in the journey.

In addition, I've listened to the experiences of thousands of people all over the world through the ministry of God Conversations. I've heard the testimonies of friends and family and leaders and pastors, as well as the questions and experiences of spiritual seekers. I've also researched the dreams and visions of the biblical characters through my PhD studies. And this is what I've observed: times haven't changed much since the time of Job; God may well be speaking, but many of us still struggle to recognize it.

The aim of this book is to help provide a solution. Specifically, the book is designed to help you recognize God's voice in his most favoured form: dreams and visions. God hasn't changed his communication methods since the time of the Bible. He is still speaking in dreams and visions, but too often we miss them. There are reasons for this. Some of them are historical – the legacy of old mindsets that reject any sort of supernatural or spiritual experience. Some of them are theological – the outcome of distorted ideas that haven't been properly reconciled in our different church traditions. Some of them are practical – we simply don't understand how dreams and visions work, we're fearful of getting it wrong, or we've experienced too much abuse in this area from those around us. We will explore all of these and more in this book.

God Dreams is divided into two parts. The first part deals with the nature of dreams and visions. We will look at what they are, why God uses them to speak and where they come from. Here we draw on the fields of psychology, neuroscience and world religions in addition to the Christian Scriptures. While dream interpretation is more art than science, we gain much from the work of psychologists and neuroscientists. The goal is to see the bigger picture and gain wisdom from those who have gone before. Through it all, our main reference point is Jesus and his continuing mission through the Holy Spirit.

In the second part of the book, we explore the practicalities – how to understand dreams and visions and the language of symbolism. Here we delve into the best examples of visual God-conversations from the time of the New Testament church, beginning with Peter's vision of an unappetizing lunch in the early years of the first century and ending with John's visions in the latter years. Understanding the creativity and efficacy of the Spirit's communication in these visions provides profound insights into our own. You will gain an understanding of what dreams and visions are, where they come from, and how to know when they're from God. You will learn how picture language and symbols work. You will understand why the Spirit speaks and how to respond when he does.

My prayer in writing this book is that you, the reader, will appreciate the beauty and power of your own dream-visions. Having experienced the startling revelation that came from unravelling my own, I am convinced that you too will be surprised by their creativity, wisdom and encouragement. Most of all, I pray that you will hear the voice of God in them.

God is speaking! His words are full of revelation and power. God speaks in order to invite us into relationship and partnership with his plan. Dreams and visions may well be the easiest way to hear from God. All it takes is a heart to know God and a good night's sleep.

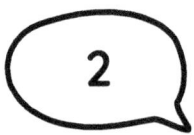

What Are Dreams and Visions?

I Believe I Can Fly

Some of my favourite dreams are the ones where I'm flying. Each dream has its own variation, but I'm always left with little doubt: I really *can* fly. Typically, they begin with me launching off the side of a building or from the centre of a grassy field. I take off with gusto, soaring confidently into the air. From high above, I can see the rooftops of skyscrapers, roads curling around like spaghetti, and people like tiny ants crawling up and down the paths. There's always a thrilling sense of power and joy. I know that when I wake up, I'll be able to do it again.

But then of course, I do wake up and I can't do it again. The disappointment is real. I've had flying dreams since I was a child, and every time, they leave me with the same sense of exhilaration followed by crushing disappointment.

Another common theme of my dreams is the mission to find a toilet. Far less pleasant than my escapades above the rooftops, these dreams usually catch me in a desperate search for the loo. When I eventually find one, I can't use it. The reasons are varied – the bathroom door is locked, the toilet bowl is filthy, or there's no privacy – but the ever-present sense of desperation is the same. When I eventually open my eyes, I find myself sprinting for the bathroom, thankful I've woken in time. As someone once said, 'If you see a toilet in your dream, don't use it!'

There have been other dreams too. These have had little to do with bodily functions or repressed desires. Instead, they seem to arise from another world. They are dreams where I've seen the house I would come to live in, places I would later visit and people I would meet in real life soon after. Sometimes they have been stunningly precise in their detail. When they've eventually played themselves out, the feeling has been surreal and otherworldly – a kind of pinch-yourself moment, followed by a questioning of your sanity. These dreams are relatively rare, but each time, they have overwhelmed me with their mystery and marked me with their power.

Research tells us that I am not alone in my dreaming. In particular, visions of flying and toileting are common. Frequently our dreams contain elements that hark back to our waking lives, but there are plenty of unusual stories too. History tells of those who have experienced flashes of otherworldly insight while they slept. Albert Einstein's theory of relativity, Mary Shelley's plot for *Frankenstein*, Salvador Dali's design of *Persistence of Memory*, and the melody for Paul McCartney's song 'Yesterday' were all said to have been inspired by a dream. Others have seen premonitions of death in their dreams – either of others or of themselves, Abraham Lincoln and Mark Twain being some of the best-known examples.

No doubt you have your own stories to tell. Dreams range from the fanciful to the literal, the mundane to the creative, and the natural to the supernatural. They can exist as a single image, an isolated scene or an elaborate story. Many are muddy and chaotic. Sometimes, they are wildly embarrassing. Most seem useless and, for the most part, not worth remembering. They are like the fragments of your past tossed together in a colourful salad, where you wake up thinking, *What on earth did I eat last night?* But then occasionally, you find yourself experiencing a strangely coherent dream; it lingers long into the day and seems to call you to ponder.

What are dreams and visions? What purpose do they have? Historically, the western world hasn't bothered much with these questions, but in the last fifty years or so, interest has risen exponentially.[1] Studies in dreaming have become popular across a variety of disciplines, giving us much to work with. The scientific world offers us insights into the physicality of dreams and visions through studies of the brain. Psychology teaches us how we can use dreams as a vehicle for personal growth. Religion and spirituality present dreams as a doorway into the spiritual realm and the means through which angels, demons and spirits communicate. The Hebrew-Christian Scriptures tell us that dreams can be the voice of God.

Our understanding of hearing God's voice in dreams and visions is enhanced when we explore the phenomenon as a whole. In this chapter, we take a closer look at the dream experience through a range of lenses. We begin with the insights of neuroscience.

Neuroscience: Our Brains at Work

Have you ever watched someone while they sleep? Sometimes, their eyelids flutter and a sudden tremor ripples through their bodies. At other times, there is no movement at all. What is happening to our physical bodies when we dream?

Neuroscience, or more specifically, the field of 'oneirology', provides us with some answers. These insights are made possible through the use of a machine called the electroencephalogram (EEG). First invented in the 1950s, the EEG measures the electrical activity of our brains and offers a wealth of insight into the physicality of dreaming.

We learn from EEGs that when we dream, our bodies and minds get busy. Our eyelids begin to ripple as our eyes move rapidly beneath them, and our brain waves change from the random zigzag of sleep to a flattened, low-voltage pattern, almost like attentive waking. There are metabolic changes too. Our heartbeat, blood pressure and breathing are all roused from the slow, even rhythms of sleep to suddenly speed up or slow down.[2] During the dreaming phase of sleep, our bodies also experience a temporary form of paralysis (perhaps to prevent us acting out our dreams).

Scientists tell us that these processes happen to all of us. *Everybody* dreams, whether they know it or not. When people say they don't have dreams, it's simply because they don't remember them.[3] EEGs tell us that even unborn babies and animals dream![4]

It has been calculated that we all dream for 1–2 hours a night in a regular pattern. Something is going on practically all the time in sleep, while about every 90 minutes a vivid dream occurs. That makes for an average of four to five dreaming periods a night.[5]

Our most active dreaming occurs during the stage of sleep known as 'rapid eye movement' (REM). REM periods can last for a few minutes to over an hour, increasing successively during the night. It is during this stage of sleep that the levels of certain neurotransmitters are elevated, contributing to our sense that the dream is real.[6] We find ourselves convinced that we really can fly! Indeed, we are more likely to remember our dreams when we are woken directly after REM sleep.

We also learn that during the dream state, certain parts of our brains are more active than others. It shouldn't be surprising that these are the areas that are responsible for telling stories and experiencing emotions, with the verbal and logical areas less so.

Neuroscientists also tell us that dreaming functions as a normal part of our bodily processes and contributes significantly to our physical development. As we sleep, dreams help to restore key neurotransmitters and repair mechanisms in our brains, even helping to consolidate memories and skills. As the logic of our waking lives is suspended, the brain works to solve problems, discard useless thoughts and help us perform mental tasks so that we do better when we wake. In other words, dreaming helps us to think clearly in our waking lives. When faced with a problem, the call to 'sleep on it' seems to have scientific merit![7]

The insights of neuroscience mean that we can appreciate the important role dreaming plays in our cognitive development. But what do our dreams mean? For that, we turn to the work of psychologists.

Psychology: A Shadow of Ourselves

Most of us in the West tend to assume that our dreams are meaningless – the mere product of pizza for dinner the night before. Since they are just the random 'leftovers' of our memories, activities and emotions, they should be ignored. 'It's just a dream,' we say. While there is *some* evidence to suggest that certain foods may affect our dreams,[8] psychologists tell us there is more to dreams than just a spicy meal. The field of psychology focuses on the meaning of dreams and their relationship to our emotional and psychological development.

Caught on a microwave

Aaron is a friend with a big-hearted wife and two active children. A few years ago, he took on the role of househusband while his wife focused on growing her career. Around this time, Aaron had a dream. He saw himself surfing at a local beach. Just as he was about to catch a wave, he felt his leg pulling him downwards under the water. When he looked to find out what it was, he discovered that the leg rope from his surfboard was caught on a microwave oven.

When I asked Aaron if he felt 'caught between' his domestic duties and leisure time, he started laughing: 'Yes! I've been stressing about all the things I have to do – cleaning the house, dropping the kids at school and ironing uniforms, while my wife keeps telling me to chill out and watch TV.'

Aaron's dream is a good example of how dreams may offer us more than a jumbled kaleidoscope of irrelevant and unrelated images. His dream revealed the tensions Aaron was experiencing in his waking life and pointed towards resolution and wholeness. This dynamic of dreams has been explored by psychologists. They tell us that dreaming plays an important role in our mental and emotional development.

One of the reasons psychologists have made this conclusion is because of what happens when dreaming is interrupted. Studies show that if people are woken up just before entering REM sleep, they make persistent attempts to make up for the loss by re-entering the dream state. Then, when people are consistently deprived of dreaming, they begin to show signs of mental breakdown! A lack of concentration, depletion in memory and motor control, moderate anxiety, mood swings and weight gain have all been shown to occur when individuals are deprived of dreaming.[9] When that deprivation is prolonged, it can even lead to psychotic manifestations. It is no wonder that Dr William Dement, who first studied dreams in the 1960s, called them the 'very guardians of sanity'.[10] Humans *need* to dream! Dreaming keeps us emotionally and mentally healthy.

Psychology also focuses on the content of our dreams through psychoanalysis. It may come as no surprise that the content of our dreams is most often linked to the issues we are experiencing in our waking life. The 'consistency hypothesis' says that the more we think about certain topics by day, the more they will feature in our dreams at night.[11] The most common themes seem to involve 'distraction', such as missing buses, searching for toilets, experiences of falling, losing teeth, appearing naked in public or being chased.

However, dreams seem to have more to say than just a rehash of the previous day's events. Often, they unfold with a goal in mind. For example, several studies point to the purpose of dreams and visions towards the end of our lives. In one North American study, 90% of patients in the sample told of how dreams helped them to accept their impending death.[12] Many of their dreams featured living friends and family members and pointed to the resolution of conflict. As death approached, people also saw deceased loved ones waiting for them. Researchers found that dreams consistently brought comfort and peace and lessened the fear of dying. Dreams like these reveal a psychological function to our dreaming. Perhaps they are not as random as we think.

Early dream analysts

The idea that our dreams have psychological significance was first explored by Sigmund Freud in 1899 in his book, *The Interpretation of Dreams*. His work was later built upon by Swiss psychologist Carl Jung.[13] Both Freud and Jung came to understand dreams to be a window into the subconscious personality. Like shadows reflecting a reality we don't always see, dreams can give us insight into what is happening beneath the surface of our lives. We may not even be aware of the thoughts and feelings in our waking lives, but they will likely surface in our dreams. Dreams are the great revealer! So, we dream of turning up naked to an examination when we're anxious about a big performance review the next day. We dream of being chased down a dead-end alley when we're faced with the stress of having no options. Or we dream of being caught on a microwave when we're struggling to balance our recreational and domestic priorities.

As we know, dreams speak an unusual language. Messages about being caught between two concerns come packaged as a surfboard tied down by a microwave oven! Both Freud and Jung acknowledged the place of symbols and imagery in dreams but came to different conclusions about them. Freud argued that the reason dreams speak symbolically is because we *don't want* to hear them. The messages of our dreams are 'obnoxious' and must therefore be translated into a more acceptable form: 'The unconscious wishes to speak and to express its desires and meaning, but it is impeded from this by the conscious actions of the dreamer. Much of the dream material is obnoxious to the conscious personality unless it is distorted.'[14] Thus, Freud might say that Aaron didn't *want* to confront the dilemma of his dual priorities – his conscious-self censored the message from his unconscious-self by disguising it in symbolism.

Carl Jung had a different idea. He argued that the unconscious mind thinks metaphorically and symbolically to begin with. That is, dreaming draws on the language of art, literature, mythology and folklore, imagination and religion. For Jung, our challenge is that we *do not know* this language very well since we're more familiar with the world of rationalism, logic and science. Dreams show what happens when our rational thinking is switched off, providing renewed ways of understanding ourselves.

Psychologists offer many helpful insights into the dream life, some of which we will explore further in Chapter 5. But there is more to dreams than the operation of the psyche. Dreams can venture into the world of the paranormal, where we experience the presence of other spirits and catch a glimpse into the unknown. Even Jung acknowledged that dreams may offer insights that transcend a person's conscious knowledge and attitude,[15] and several contemporary studies verify the reality of 'telepathic' or 'psychic' dreams. Indeed, these types of 'supernatural' dreams may be more common than we realize.[16] Here our discussion takes us into the world of religion and spirituality.

Religion and Spirituality: Doorways to Another Realm

Could the gods be speaking to us in our dreams? For nearly every culture of the world apart from the modern West, the answer is *yes*. From Ancient Egypt and the Near East to China, India and the Australian Aboriginals and Torres Strait Islanders, people have believed that another world of reality beyond the physical breaks in on people through dreams. This spiritual world involves the activity of gods, goddesses, demons and angels. For religious historian Mircea Eliade, there is 'hardly a culture on earth that has not shared this interest in dreams'.[17] Religion and spirituality teach us that dreams can act as a means of communicating with spirit beings, thus providing a bridge between the natural and supernatural realm.

The belief in dreams as a doorway into the spiritual realm is seen throughout ancient literature. Documents from as far back as the third millennium BCE tell of their importance. From the Egyptians, we find papyri giving instructions on how to obtain a dream-vision from the gods, and a dream book listing over a hundred common dreams and their meanings. From the Semitic cultures of Asia Minor and the Trans-Euphrates in the early third millennium BCE, we read about dreams providing direction from the gods to leading heroes, as in the famed *Epic of Gilgamesh*. From the Ancient Greeks, we learn about the role of dreams in Homer's *Iliad* of the eighth century BCE, and from the Assyrians, how the goddess Ishtar communicated to the king in a dream. Finally, from the Ancient Babylonians, we discover that dream interpretation was part of the job description for the 'wise men' of the royal court (Dan. 2:1–13). Indeed, from all over the Ancient Near East, we find books and manuscripts that helped people interpret their dreams.[18]

The ancients also saw a connection between dreams and healing. As far back as the fourth century BCE, Hippocrates, the father of modern medicine, used dreams as a diagnostic tool. The Greeks in particular understood that the psyche and the body interacted closely with each other. Indeed, the use of dreams for healing (known as 'incubation') was practised in many of the Greek temples. If unwell, an Ancient Greek would stay overnight in the temple's dedicated sleep sanctuary, anticipating that Asclepius, the god of medicine, would visit them in their dreams. Next morning, they would expect to either wake up cured or be given a diagnosis from the priest based on his interpretation of their dream.

From the West, we move to the East, where the spiritual value of dreams also features prominently. In the Hindu Upanishads of India, dreams were understood to bring illumination from the spirit realm and contribute to enlightenment. The Ancient Chinese (sixth and seventh centuries CE) also valued dreams, with two chief dream books, *Meng Shu* and *Meng Chan I Chih*, offering plentiful instruction.

Dreams also feature regularly in the teachings of Buddhism. The very beginning of the life of its founder, Siddhartha

Gautama (567–487 BCE), was marked by a dream. In the dream, Siddhartha's mother saw her side being pierced by the tusk of a six-tusked elephant. She understood it meant her child would become a monarch who would rule the world. The Buddhist scriptures go on to mention five of the Buddha's dreams.

Into the sixth century CE, the dreaming tradition continued in the Muslim world, with Muhammad, the founder of Islam, claiming his teachings came directly in visions from the angel Gabriel. Today, Muslims still value the spiritual dynamic of dreams and have their own book of dream interpretations called *Kitab al-Ahlam*. They also celebrate the 'night of power' (*Laylat ul-Qadr*) during Ramadan when the faithful expect to hear God's voice in a dream.

Finally, dreaming features prominently in many of the indigenous tribal cultures of the world. The work of anthropologists has shown the spiritual importance of dreams among peoples from Africa, India and North America to Australia and Papua New Guinea.[19]

The ancient perspective on dreaming as an interface between the spiritual and natural realms also formed the backdrop of Israel's story, Jesus' life and the early church. Dreams and visions were a common presence in the Ancient Hebrew and Greco-Roman world. It is to the Judeo-Christian perspective on dreaming that we now turn.

The Scriptures: The Voice of God

In the first book of the Scriptures, we read a pivotal story from the life of one of Israel's leading figures. The young man is far from home and running from his family. Though raised in a privileged household, his journey had been marked by deceit and confusion. Now, it seemed, he was paying the price. Isolated and rejected in the middle of a desert, he falls asleep and has a dream. In his dream, he sees a number of angels moving up and down a great stairway. The stairway touches the earth and reaches far into the heavens.

The man was Jacob, son of Isaac, son of Abraham. In his dream, he had heard a voice, reminding him of his legacy and calling him to a different future. On waking, Jacob recognized the presence of God: 'Surely the LORD is in this place, and I was not aware of it' (Gen. 28:10–22). Jacob's story shows how the Scriptures share the ancient perspective on dreaming as a doorway into the spiritual realm.

Jacob's story is not an isolated one. In the Bible, we see that dreams and visions are often the voice of the Creator God. They are God's 'modus operandi' – his *normal mode* of communication.[20] There are so many dreams and visions in the Bible that it is difficult to count them. As we've seen, one author has suggested they constitute a third of the Hebrew Scriptures (the Old Testament).[21]

Biblical scholars tell us that under both the Old and New Covenants, all God-conversations are categorized as dreams and visions. Even aural experiences with no visual element are subsumed in this grouping (e.g. Acts 9:10; 10:19), though logically it makes little sense![22] Angels too, are included,[23] with an angel often described as 'appearing in' a vision or dream (e.g. Zech. 1:8–9; Matt. 1:20; Acts 10:3).

God himself describes dreams and visions as his main form of speaking early on in biblical history: 'I, the LORD, reveal myself to them [the prophets] in visions, I speak to them in dreams' (Num. 12:6b; also Hos. 12:10). Under the Old Covenant, God would reveal his message largely to the prophets, who would then 'prophesy' or *pass them on* to God's people. In fact, the original word in Hebrew for 'prophet' was 'seer'.[24] Prophets *saw* what God was saying in dreams and visions. As the prophet Jeremiah described it, you could both *hear* and *see* God's word (Jer. 23:18a).

As the biblical stories unfold, we discover that hearing God in dreams and visions was the experience of all the main biblical characters. Abraham, Moses, Jacob, Ezekiel, Jeremiah, Zechariah, and many others, all heard God speak in this way. As we've seen, one of the oldest books of the Bible states it clearly: 'For God does speak – now one way, now another . . . In a dream, in a vision of the night' (Job 33:14–15). It seems that this expectation was true for much of biblical history. When King Saul, for example, sought to hear from God, he anticipated it would come in one of two ways: 'by prophets or by dreams' (1 Sam. 28:15b).[25] Biblically, hearing God's voice in dreams and visions was the norm.

So we read how Abraham dreamed of a blazing torch that passed between animal sacrifices as a way of sealing God's covenant with him (Gen. 15); Jacob dreamed of a stairway to heaven that transformed his life (Gen. 28:10–17); and Joseph's future was illumined through a dream of sun, moon and stars bowing down in deference (Gen. 37:9–10).

Then, as the nation of Israel formed, God-dreams led the nation into the period of the judges and kings, with Gideon's dream of the barley loaf (Judg. 7:13–14), Micaiah's vision of the heavenly council (1 Kgs 22:19–28) and Solomon's request for wisdom (1 Kgs 3:5–15).

Later, dreams and visions feature prominently in the ministry of the prophets. Amos experienced a vision of a basket of summer fruit representing the state of Israel (Amos 8). Isaiah saw a throne on high, commissioning him into his calling (Isa. 6), and Jeremiah envisaged the coming troubles of his era as a boiling pot (Jer. 1:13–16). Dream-visions also feature in the time of the Jewish exile, with Daniel's dreams of four beasts depicting the rise and fall of foreign empires (Dan. 7), Ezekiel's valley of dry bones (Ezek. 37:1–14) and Zechariah's vision of two olive trees and a golden lampstand (Zech. 4).

When we move into the New Testament, God's favoured form of communication continues. Jesus himself experienced God's voice in a vision of a dove at his baptism (Matt. 3:16–17) and later at the Transfiguration with the appearance of Moses and Elijah (Matt. 17:1–9).

Then as the early church is birthed on the Day of Pentecost, we see God's visual form of communication increasing exponentially as everyone is given full access to the Holy Spirit. According to the apostle Peter, this was the fulfilment of the Old Covenant promise that God would pour out his Spirit on all people:

> Your sons and daughters will prophesy,
> > your young men will see visions,
> > your old men will dream dreams.

Acts 2:17, quoting Joel 2:28

No longer did you need to be a prophet to hear God's voice – everyone could hear from God directly! And so the pattern continues, from the Old Covenant into the New: God speaks in dreams and visions and the message is passed on as prophecy.

Following the monumental events of Pentecost, the truth of Peter's proclamation manifested in the life of the early church. New Testament scholar John Miller counts over twenty instances of God speaking in dreams and visions in the book of Acts.[26] Each time the Spirit spoke, it brought life-changing impact to God's people. Morton Kelsey observes that every major event in Acts is marked by a dream, a vision, or the appearance of an angel, and it is usually 'upon this experience that the coming events are determined'.[27]

Of course, the testimony of Scripture also indicates that not all dreams and visions come from the Creator God. Scripture warns of false dreams, and dreams that arise from our own hearts (Jer. 23:16) or from other spirits. This is why all dream-visions had to be tested to determine if they were from God (Deut. 18:10–13; 1 John 4:1). Only then were they to be followed.

Types of dream-visions

The experience of dreams and visions can be difficult to put into words since everyone encounters them differently. In the past, some have attempted to categorize *types* of dreams and visions based on the biblical experience. The challenge is that Scripture doesn't provide us with clear and consistent terminology.

In our time, we tend to differentiate between a dream and a vision by the dreamer's level of consciousness – so we have a 'dream' when we're asleep and a 'vision' when we're awake. But in the original language of Scripture, the terms for dreams and visions were interchangeable and there is no clear defining line between them[28] (e.g. Num. 12:6; Joel 2:28). This is why scholars often use the term 'dream-visions'[29] in their discussions (as do I in this book). What's more, a dream is often described in Scripture as a 'vision of the night' (e.g. Gen. 46:2; Job 4:13; 20:8; 33:15; Isa. 29:7; Dan. 2:19).[30] The emphasis is on the *visual* quality of the experience rather than the state of a person's consciousness.

We see this merging of terminology in Abraham's life, when God spoke about his future as the father of a nation that would bring great blessing to the world. At first, we read that God spoke when Abraham was awake, but soon after, the account says he was asleep (Gen. 15)! So was it a vision or a dream? In another key God-conversation in Scripture, God spoke to the apostle Peter about the Gentiles while he was 'in a trance'; was he awake or asleep – or perhaps somewhere in between?

Another way of categorizing dream-visions is by the degree to which a person enters the spiritual realm. So, someone may have an 'open vision' whereby they are admitted into the spiritual world and experience its effects externally and physically. Or they may have a 'closed vision,' in which they remain in the natural world and experience the spiritual realm internally with minimal physical effects. The Old Covenant prophet Ezekiel and the early church leader John both seemed to have experienced an open vision when they were relocated 'in the Spirit' and saw scenes of heavenly creatures (Ezek. 1:1; Rev. 1). Similarly, the early church martyr Stephen was given special access into an 'open' heaven as he passed from the natural to the spiritual realm in death (Acts 7:55–56).

What Are Dreams and Visions?

At other times, God's heavenly messengers appear to move in the opposite direction – from the spiritual to the natural realm. This occurred with the appearance of angels in Jacob's dream (Gen. 28:10–22), Joseph's vision about Mary's pregnancy (Matt. 2:13) and in Peter's prison cell (Acts 12:7–10), as well as in the appearance of Moses and Elijah at Jesus' transfiguration (Matt. 17:1–8). In dream-visions, the boundary between the physical and the spiritual world is porous, inviting easy passage between the two.

In everyday life, intense, otherworldly visionary experiences are rare. In the Bible, they seem to feature more regularly because Scripture acts as a sort of 'highlight reel' to God's story. The Bible writers focus on significant moments that mark God's overt participation in history. While we may have our own 'highlight reels' or life-changing experiences, in everyday life, the vast majority of our visionary experiences are more likely to happen *internally*, with the Spirit's voice experienced in 'quieter' and more subtle ways. Or, as Daniel described it, they come by 'passing through' our minds (see Dan. 4:5; also Dan. 7:1).

Whatever the level of intensity, physicality or consciousness in our dream-visions, the consistent message of Scripture is that God may be speaking. The focus is always on the message over the medium. Whether spectacular or mundane, a genuine Spirit-inspired dream-vision offers us a life-changing glimpse into God's heart and his plan for our lives.

* * *

Dream-visions are inherently complex and mysterious, calling us to be cautious about making definitive statements about them. Yet there is much we can know. From neuroscience, we learn of the workings of our brains as we sleep and that dreaming provides a process of restoration that is integral to our physical health. From psychology, we learn that dreaming can bring self-awareness and point us towards wholeness. From religion and spirituality, we learn that the spirit realm may be active as we sleep. And from Judeo-Christian history, we learn that the God of the Bible uses dream-visions to reveal his character and purpose.

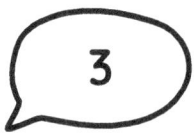

The Language of Dream-Visions

A Floating Caravan

In the summer of 2003, I moved interstate to Sydney from my home in Melbourne. It was an exciting but tumultuous time, especially when it came to finding a permanent place to live. For a wearying two years, I unpacked and repacked, boxed and re-boxed my belongings, shuffling them across the city a total of seven times.

It seemed things had finally settled when I moved into a two-bed apartment on Sydney's north shore. The flat was clean and functional, within easy driving distance to work, and came with a reliable flatmate. Here, it seemed, I could finally set up home.

So that's what I attempted to do. Most of my larger pieces of furniture were still back in Melbourne, so I made the most of what I had, camouflaging packing boxes with strategically placed cloths and ornaments, sorting my clothing on makeshift racks and hiding extraneous items from sight. Afterwards, the space looked comfortable and homey. I surveyed it with a smile, went to bed, and fell into a contented sleep.

That night, I had a dream. In the dream, I saw a caravan floating down a fast-flowing muddy river. I was inside the caravan, trying to keep it clean. But there was a problem. The water from the river kept flowing in through the caravan door. I would sweep it out and it would flow back in . . . sweep it out and flow back in . . . over and over again. Frustration mounted to fever pitch as my efforts were continually stifled by the never-ending stream of dirty water. All the while, I wondered: *Why am I living in a caravan? And why is it floating on a river?*

A few days later, my new flatmate announced her engagement. I would have to move. Again.

I shouldn't have been surprised. After all, a caravan is a *portable* home. Caravans are always on the move – and even more so, if found on a fast-flowing river! Clever, isn't it? Though it wasn't welcome news, the dream prophesied my situation perfectly.

A message in pictures

Dream-visions speak a unique language. They employ the imagery of animals, objects and people to communicate a message. In this strange world of symbols and pictures, people can fly, animals can speak and caravans can float on muddy rivers. Of course, sometimes dream-visions do contain words, but mostly they come as a colourful kaleidoscope of scenes, imagery and emotions. Once you understand how they work, you realize what a powerful form of communication they can be.

Consider one of the most famous dreams of the ancient biblical world. This dream went on to direct the economic policy of the greatest empire of the day.

The Language of Dream-Visions 33

Can you see it?

> A cow emerges from a river. It's strong and fat with a glossy coat and bright eyes. A second cow soon follows, its tail swinging in the breeze. Then another and another; five, six and seven. Seven bountiful creatures grazing happily among the reeds.
>
> Soon after, another cow appears. This cow is different. Its ribs protrude offensively, and its eyes are gaunt as it stumbles up the bank. As before, a second cow follows, then another. Eventually, seven miserable creatures join the seven fat cows loitering along the riverbank in search of food.
>
> Suddenly there's a commotion in the herd. A flurry of hooves stirs the mud and water in a hunting frenzy. When the reeds clear and the blood settles, only seven cows remain. The glossy fat cows are no longer. The skinny cattle have eaten their fill. But strangely they are as gaunt as ever.
> *Adapted from Gen. 41:1–4*

The dream of the fat and skinny cows belonged to the Egyptian pharaoh at the time of Joseph when the nation of Israel was still only an idea. A second dream had followed. This time, seven healthy ears of corn were consumed by seven thin ears of corn (Gen. 41:5–7).

At the time of Pharaoh's dreams, Egypt was known as the breadbasket of the Mediterranean and the majority of the then-known world relied on it for its grain supply. After the dream was interpreted (by Joseph), it went on to inform economic policy for the next fourteen years.

Just as my dream of the floating caravan conveyed a message in pictures familiar to my life, the pharaoh's dream used imagery based on the agricultural setting of his life. The seven fat cows represented seven years of plenty, and the seven skinny cows represented seven years of drought. The drought would follow the years of prosperity and would be so severe as to swallow up the abundance of the years that preceded it. Understanding the symbolism of the dream allowed the rulers of Egypt to take action to avert the effects of the drought (Gen. 41:1–56). Such is the nature of dreams. Objects, animals, scenes and even people are used to represent something else. They act as a rhetorical device – a kind of *language* if you like.

This language of symbolism is often intensely dramatic. Dreams appear larger than life, like scenes on steroids. Feelings, thoughts and problems take on exaggerated form in the theatre of our minds. Fear becomes a monster, hope becomes a sunrise, and limitation becomes a coat that's too small to fit in.

As we've seen, Sigmund Freud argued that dreams employ symbols as a type of disguise because we don't want to hear their message. Carl Jung, on the other hand, argued that picture language is used because it's how we inherently think (even when we're unaware of it). The language of dream-visions may appear strange and unfamiliar at first, but once we understand it, the mystery clears. We come to appreciate the power of visual imagery to speak to the deepest parts of ourselves.

In this chapter, we explore the nature of dream-vision language in detail. We outline the need for interpretation, and the difference between literal and symbolic dream-visions. We also suggest reasons why God might prefer dream-visions over other modes of communication.

The Art of Interpretation

Because dream-visions speak the language of symbols and imagery, they require interpretation. At first, the message may appear random or obscure, but this is usually because we don't understand how imagery works. Like any language, it can be learned. But this is not as difficult as it first seems. After all, pictures are the most basic of languages. They are *preverbal*. When we first teach children to read, what do we give them? It's not the Oxford dictionary!

The truth is that we use symbols all the time, even when we're not aware of it. A coloured light signals when to step on the brakes in our car, a red cross directs us to the source of medical help, and a hand signal relays peace. They all do this effectively – without words. Symbols form a universal language that transcends the barriers of communication.

This means that dream-visions are like a puzzle to work out or, as Scripture describes them, a 'riddle' to be solved (Num. 12:8). They are not unlike Jesus' parables. Once we understand how they work, they are more easily deciphered.

Think back to the pharaoh's dreams of the cows and ears of corn. At first, their meaning was unclear to the pharaoh, and he turned to Joseph for help. Joseph was familiar with the language of dreams and knew that they required interpretation to be understood (Gen. 41:15–16). In some dream-visions of Scripture, an angel does the interpretation (e.g. Dan. 7:15–16; Rev. 10:8–11; 17:1–3,7–18; 19:9–10; 21:9–14; 22:1–6,8–9). In each case, we see that dream interpretation involves a certain level of expertise. But like any language, it can be developed with time and practice.

Symbolic or Literal?

Of course, not all our dreams are symbolic. Some dreams can present a literal scene, offering us a snapshot of the future, or a glimpse of reality that would normally be inaccessible. The story of my mum's dream of my grandfather is a good example.

Grandpa lived in the retirement village just down the road from my mum. After my Grandma's death a few years earlier, Grandpa had moved out of his three-bedroom home and into a small apartment, where he found a host of new friends from the retirement community. Mum visited nearly every day, dropping in with a bag of groceries and a cup of tea. Sometimes on Sundays, Grandpa would join the rest of the family as we gathered at Mum's house, diving into her famed roast dinner together. After we'd all eaten our fill, Grandpa would head back home, hunker down in his favourite recliner chair, and fall fast asleep. We would often laugh about him snoring in his chair with his mouth wide open.

One night my mum had a dream. She saw Grandpa in a familiar position – lying in his reclining chair with his mouth wide open. But this time, he wasn't snoring. Grandpa had died.

The Language of Dream-Visions　　37

In the dream, Mum prayed: 'God, please don't let me be the one to find him there.' Then she woke up.

A few days later, Mum was hosting an engagement party for my brother and his fiancée at our family home. The decorations were hung, the table was laid, and guests had begun arriving. But Grandpa wasn't among them. This was unusual – Grandpa was always on time. So my uncle offered to go down to his apartment and check on him.

No answer came when my uncle knocked on Grandpa's door. So he went round to the back of the flat and broke in. There in the lounge was Grandpa . . . lying in his favourite chair with his mouth wide open. But he wasn't snoring. Grandpa had died.

Afterwards, my mum spoke of the deep sense of peace and comfort that stayed with her because of the dream through the days leading up to the funeral and weeks later, as she helped pack up Grandpa's home. In her grief, she knew that this was God's time for her father, and it was going to be okay.

Through a dream, God had shown my mum a *literal* glimpse of the future. There was no symbolism or need for interpretation. The message had been clear.

We see another example of a more literal dream in the experience of the early church. The apostle Paul was on his second missionary journey when he faced an important decision: should he turn west or east? At first, he went towards the east – into Bithynia – but didn't feel right about it. Then he had the dream: a 'man from Macedonia' appeared and beckoned him for help (Acts 16:9). So, the next morning, Paul and his team packed up their bags and turned west towards Macedonia. Even though they didn't know specifically *who* the man was (perhaps they met him later), the message was clear and required no interpretation.

For the most part, literal dreams such as these are relatively rare. The vast majority of our dreams are symbolic. They tend to feature skinny cows and floating caravans more than a grandfather on his chair. Though they require interpretation, they can be just as powerful.

Why Dream-Visions?

Why does God speak in dream-visions? Why not just speak plainly? God could simply say: 'Pharaoh, there are seven years of drought coming, so you need to store up seven years of grain supplies', or 'Tania, don't bother settling into this apartment because you'll soon be moving house again.' Why would God shroud his message in imagery and symbolism?

Scripture doesn't explicitly give an answer, but there are probably good reasons for it, since God uses dream-visions so frequently. As a master communicator, we would expect that God would select the most effective method to get his message across.

1. The power of a picture

The answer to why God speaks in dream-visions may become clearer when we return to the insights of neuroscience. Here

The Language of Dream-Visions

we learn that visual imagery is one of the most effective tools of communication. It has been said that messages containing imagery are six and a half times more likely to stay with us than those without them![1] That's why advertisers and marketers love them. A picture really does paint a thousand words!

But there may be more to it than just getting a message across. Dream-visions usually place an idea into the context of a story. This has even greater impact on our brains. MRI scans tell us that when we watch a story unfold, we process it as *participants* rather than spectators. Not only does the dream engage the language part of our brains, but it activates the parts we would normally use if we were experiencing the events in real life.[2] What's more, when we see images in our mind, the chemicals associated with emotions are released into our bodies. This has an impact on our neural pathways and physiology. It effectively *changes us*. The effect is felt throughout our bodies, emotions and minds.

Of course, you probably know this already. You wake up from a dream feeling like you've actually been there. You really believe you can fly! You feel the terror of being chased and the palpable relief when you wake up in safety. You feel the jubilation of receiving a longed-for gift and the disappointment later when you realize it was only a dream. We enter the story and see it; we hear it and feel it. Then we are changed by it. The effect is long-lasting.

You can sense the profound impact of a dream-vision in many of our famous biblical accounts. Take the prophet Ezekiel's experience back in the sixth century BCE. At the time, the people of Israel were exiled in Babylon, far from their home. Feeling powerless and isolated, they despaired of any return. So how did God encourage them? He could have used words: 'I will restore your hopes and return you to your land.' But he didn't. Instead, he showed Ezekiel a scene:

> There's a desolate and lonely valley. All along the valley floor lies an array of bones. They've been there so long, they're dry and brittle, bleached white by the sun.
>
> Suddenly a blast of air stirs on the horizon. It swirls and blows across the valley, sweeping away the dust and exposing the bones. In response, the bones begin to shake and tremble. Joints lock together and seal, clicking in rhythmic flow. From the scatter comes order. From the dust comes alignment.
>
> Gradually flesh begins to appear. Muscle and tissue envelop the bones, finding curvature and form. Limbs and torsos, toes and fingers all take shape on the valley floor.
>
> Still the bodies lie, helpless in the void, until a final breath of wind surges through them and they rise with strength and fortitude. Together they stand in formation and resolve.
>
> *Adapted from Ezek. 37:1–10*

We can imagine how Ezekiel felt as he watched this vision unfold . . . the passion that would have been ignited as the army rose, and the stirring of hope that would have lingered when he awoke.

Now consider another dream-vision from a time not long after, when God's people had begun their journey back to their

The Language of Dream-Visions

homeland. After a protracted and painful season in Babylon, they were now faced with another challenge – how to restore the devastated ruins of their city and their most precious monument, the temple, representing God's presence and favour among them.

Again, in the midst of hopelessness, how did God speak? Not in words: 'I am commissioning two leaders to rebuild the temple', but rather in a scene to the prophet Zechariah:

> It's the menorah! The famed golden lampstand from the temple standing brilliantly with its seven branches curving upwards and outwards, blossoming into cups as though waiting to be filled. Two olive trees appear on either side of the lamp, towering and sturdy, like soldiers on guard.
>
> The scene zooms in on the branches of the two olive trees. From them, a golden pipe extends outward connecting them to the lampstand. Golden oil begins to flow from the olive trees through the pipes and into the seven channels, filling them one by one. The oil saturates the wicks, fuels the dryness, and ignites a warm and steady flame.
>
> *Adapted from Zech. 4*

We can imagine Zechariah seeing this vision for the first time: the deep sense of assurance upon sighting the menorah, that most precious and sacred symbol of the nation of Israel, even while, in reality, the temple furnishings were no more . . . the surge of strength when he understood the meaning of the two olive trees – God's chosen leaders, now empowered with the Spirit-anointed flame. There was indeed hope for the Jewish people; God's presence was among them after all.

Finally, consider a time much later in history, when the early church was cowering under the pressures of Rome's worldly system and the threat of persecution. Rome offered the glories of wealth, power and fame to those who bowed to the emperor and his self-centred ways, but what did God's kingdom offer to John and the churches of Asia Minor if they bowed to Jesus and committed to his self-sacrificing ways?

The Spirit could have used a simple sentence to communicate God's heart: 'I will heal you and reward you for your suffering', but again, God unveiled a scene:

> There's a river of water, clear as crystal without trace of contamination. From a source high above, it runs freely through the city, carving a wide path and refreshing everything in its wake.
>
> A parade of trees lines the riverbanks. They are strong and tall, offering shade to all who shelter beneath. The fruit of their boughs is heavy and their leaves are plump with verve, offering restoration and sustenance to all.
>
> *Adapted from Rev. 22:1–2*

John's vision came at a time when there was seemingly little reward in denying the ill-gained pleasures of Rome. In this vision, God gave his people a taste of the true kingdom and its unceasing bounty of love, joy and health.

As the master communicator, it should be no surprise that God uses dream-visions to speak. God has always taken advantage of the principles that neuroscience has more recently discovered. His visual communiqués switch on our brains, capture our imaginations and mobilize us into action. Faith is set alight as God vividly reveals his plan and invites us to enter it.

2. Sidestepping the conscious mind

A second reason God may speak to us in night-visions has to do with their ability to sidestep our conscious minds. We don't choose our dreams, nor can we usually direct them. Dreams say what they want to say. God seems to use this faculty to send a message that may not be easy to receive in our waking lives.

This is good news for those who struggle to sense the Spirit's voice in general. Psychological studies show that certain personalities are more conducive to picking up on impressions from the imagination. Artistic, creative types easily tend towards spiritual intuition, while analytical, thinking types can struggle to pick up on the spiritual cues.[3] If this is true, it seems unfair that some of us are predisposed to hearing the Spirit more easily than others – especially since the promise was for everyone to hear God's voice, irrespective of their neurological make-up (Acts 2:16–17). The solution? Dreams offer a way to communicate to even the most analytical brains among us. Everyone sleeps after all!

This ability to sidestep the conscious mind also means that God can get his message through the noise and distractions around us. When we sleep, God has our unrivalled attention. There's no television blaring, phones beeping or children crying. In dreams, God can touch us at the deepest level of ourselves without our even realizing it.

The ability of dreams to bypass our consciousness may also mean that God's messages can be heard when we don't *want* to hear them. We know that the Spirit speaks to transform us from the inside out, but this usually involves dealing with the sinful and hidden parts of ourselves. How does God cut through our selfishness, ignorance and preconceived ideas? Dreams provide the ideal mechanism!

A good example of this is found in King Nebuchadnezzar's dream at the time of the Babylonian exile (Dan. 4). Nebuchadnezzar was a man known for his oversized ego. When he demanded that his people worship a giant golden statue of himself on pain of death, Nebuchadnezzar's obnoxious pride was evident to everyone but him. As pride often does, it blinds us to reality. God's solution was to present the hard truth to Nebuchadnezzar as he slept.

The dream revealed a great tree with a vast host of animals nesting in its branches. The tree was Nebuchadnezzar's kingdom – famed for its luxurious palaces, buildings and vast territories. The animals in its branches were the thousands of citizens who had found a home and prosperity under Babylonian rule. But the dream went on to depict the tree being felled as a result of Nebuchadnezzar's pride. It was a fearful warning that gave the king the opportunity to repent of his ways. Unfortunately, the story goes that Nebuchadnezzar refused to change and the dream's final prediction came to pass twelve months later.

Another difficult God-conversation involved the apostle Peter at the beginnings of the Christian church (Acts 10). Holy Spirit had a message for Peter that involved the inclusion of non-Jews – Gentiles – into God's covenant people. God was saying: the good news of Jesus is for the whole world! But to a practising Jew, accustomed to avoiding Gentiles at all costs, this 'good' news would have been difficult to stomach. It contradicted all Peter had known – his Scriptures, his community, his faith and ultimately his identity. Perhaps it is not surprising that God placed Peter in a 'trance' to hear it! Freud may have been on to something when he argued that the messages of dreams can be obnoxious and need to come to us with subtlety. Our dreams can offer us a revelation of truth, even when we don't want to hear it.

3. The search for understanding

A final reason for God's preference for dream-visions may come down to the way we receive revelation. It relates to the question we often ask: *how* do we hear God's voice?

When it comes to the mechanism for hearing the Spirit, we typically prefer a neatly packaged formula: 'Take these three steps, spend this much time praying every day, read these passages of Scripture.' But the solution has far more to do with *being* than *doing*. It may also be one reason why God speaks to us in the language of pictures.

The language of dreams and visions invites us into pursuit. It beckons us to a posture of openness and humility. As any good teacher knows, understanding only comes when we are ready to receive it. As we seek, we find.

We see this approach in Jesus' teaching. Jesus regularly used parables to communicate his messages, often making the call for people to have 'ears to hear'. Those who received his message were those who positioned their hearts to understand and opened their minds to learn. They asked questions. They took time to engage. They wanted to know who Jesus was.

Once, Jesus was explicitly asked why he spoke in parables. In response, he talked about the 'secrets of the kingdom' and quoted two verses from Isaiah (6:9–10) describing a common attitude among people: "'Though seeing, they do not see; though hearing, they do not hear or understand." In them is fulfilled the prophecy of Isaiah: "You will be ever hearing but never understanding; you will be ever seeing but never perceiving'" (Matt. 13:13–14). It seems you can see truth naturally, but not spiritually. You can hear truth naturally, but not spiritually.

Jesus wasn't trying to be clever or elusive – he was highlighting the importance of our spiritual faculties. He was acknowledging the fact that revelation doesn't come through the natural senses of sight and hearing (1 Cor. 2:14). It comes through the Spirit, requiring openness, humility and a desire to learn. The apostle Paul refers to this posture as seeing with the 'eyes of the heart' and, as such, prays that the church will be open or 'enlightened' (Eph. 1:17–18). Indeed, the call to have 'ears to hear' and 'eyes to see' resounds through the Scriptures wherever revelation is on offer (Ezek. 3:27; Rev. 2:7; 3:18; 13:9).

Dream-visions offer us an invitation to seek truth and understanding. For those who are open to receive, they call us into pursuit: *What does it mean? What is God saying?* This is a different approach from the rational. It is a language of the heart that calls to the very deepest parts of ourselves.

The Language of Dream-Visions 47

An Unopened Letter

A young woman was sitting in the front row of one of our God Dreams seminars. I noticed her leaning in, listening intently and taking notes throughout the seminar. When we reached the second session, her eyes lit up and tears began to roll down her cheeks. When I asked what was happening, she told me about a recurring dream she'd had for years. She had never understood it, but now she did. Now she knew what to do.

A first-century rabbi once said, 'An uninterpreted dream is a letter unopened.' How many of us have letters waiting for us, yet to be read? This woman took the time to find out. She carved out half a day on her weekend, prioritized it in her calendar and came ready with eyes to see and ears to hear.

God has a tailor-made message for each of us. It will bring life, awaken us to new possibilities and call us into divine plans. It will hold answers to our questions and provide wisdom for our problems. God's communiqués are an expression of intimacy and love. They are personally addressed to us, signed with his name and sealed with his immutable intent and power.

Yet too often they remain unnoticed, like a letter in a postbox, its edges curling and ink fading . . . waiting to be opened.

Dreams and visions call us to open our hearts, ask questions and learn their language. Like any language, it can take time. But it's not out of our reach. It's the language we used as children when we first learned to read. All it requires is some attention and practice. It will be worth it.

When a Dream Is Not a Dream

Why the Strange Looks?

When I first relocated from my home town in Melbourne to Sydney, people would ask me why I'd moved. Why leave a secure job, a comfortable home, a community of great friends and all I'd ever known to come to a city that was over 600 miles away where there was no job, no home and no friends?

If you had asked me that summer when I was still adjusting to the sticky weather and the spaghetti-shaped roads, I would most likely have said it was to 'pursue a new work opportunity' or something normal-sounding like that. You would have smiled, and we would have talked about the weather and carried on.

On the other hand, you might have caught me in a more vulnerable moment. I might have looked in your eyes and sized you up as someone who could handle the real story behind why I moved: 'God spoke to me in dreams.'

Now maybe you would have clapped your hands together and said, 'Wow, that's amazing! What else did God say?' But perhaps, more likely, you'd have raised your eyebrows and changed the subject.

I knew what people were thinking in those moments. And I used to wonder as I walked away, *Should I have said that?*

So many strange looks. So many blank faces. And yet many of them from Christians who believed in the work of the Holy Spirit. Why were they so sceptical?

In my befuddlement, I would often think back to another story. Another big move. A young couple who had packed up their belongings, left their community and arrived in a foreign land, homeless and alone (Matt. 2:13–18). And I would wonder: did people raise their eyebrows at Joseph and Mary when they explained they'd moved because God had spoken to them in dreams?

Isn't it odd that when we read the Christmas story with its five God-dreams guiding all the main characters, we don't roll our eyes and walk away! And yet when it comes to similar testimonies in our day, many do. Many remain sceptical and dismissive – even though dream-visions are so prevalent in Scripture, even though they're explicitly described as legitimate forms of divine communication, and even though some of the most pivotal moments in biblical history were based on them.

These days – particularly in the western parts of the world – dream encounters are more likely to be rejected as a figment of our unreliable imagination or the result of consuming a spicy meal the night before. To consider a dream significant is often seen as weird or superstitious, or even a sign of mental instability.

Admittedly, some of our caution is well founded. When it comes to the idea of God speaking in dreams, people sometimes tend towards a kind of hyper-spirituality. They see some sort of monster in their dream and interpret it to mean Armageddon is around the corner. They obsess about every single dream, trying to find meaning in each detail.

But the main issue here is not dreams themselves, but our discernment of them. Not all dreams come from God, in the same way that not all our waking thoughts come from God. As Scripture says, dreams come when there are many cares (Eccl. 5:3), and every claim to revelation must be tested (1 John 4:1).

Even while some of our reticence towards dream-visions may be legitimate, there are bigger issues at play. These have more to do with the legacy of our western culture than with an open and honest reading of Scripture. In this chapter, we look at different views towards visionary experiences in history in order to understand how we've arrived at a place where we accept the God-dreams of the Bible, but not the God-dreams of our everyday lives.

Beyond Bible Times

We know that in biblical history, dream-visions were God's favoured mode of communication. The lives of Abraham, Jacob, Joseph, Ezekiel, Daniel, Jesus, Peter and John and many others were changed because of a visionary encounter. But what about beyond the pages of the Bible?[1]

Belief in dream-visions as a legitimate mode of divine communication continued beyond the period of the first Christian

When a Dream Is Not a Dream

communities into the next few centuries. Many of the church fathers, mothers and martyrs testified to the experience of the Spirit bringing direction in a dream. One of the most popular books of the early church, *The Shepherd of Hermas*, was full of dream-visions, and some of our most famous Christian martyrs such as Perpetua and Polycarp were sustained by dreams as they approached their executions.

We get an idea of how widespread the belief in God-dreams was in the commentary of an early church theologian from North Africa named Tertullian (160–230 CE). Known today for his writings on the Trinity, Tertullian was a theological heavyweight of his time. According to him, 'nearly everyone on earth knows that God reveals himself to people most often in dreams!'[2] Clearly, hearing from God in dreams in Tertullian's day was the norm.

Beyond the early centuries, we continue to read about the value of dream-visions by some of our most famous figures in the Western Church, including Athanasius, Ambrose and Augustine. It was similar in the East, with influential doctors of the church such as Gregory of Nyssa, Basil the Great, Gregory of Nazianzen and preacher John Chrysostom all indicating the significance of dream-visions in their writings. Many of them testified personally to the impact of visionary experiences in their lives. These leaders were well aware of the challenges in discerning God's voice in dream-visions, but it didn't stop them from appreciating them as a potential source of divine revelation.

However, not all leaders in the post-biblical period were as inclined towards dream-visions. For some, the misuse and abuse of visionary experiences led to their rejection, along with the development of a theology to support their position. One of the most prominent objectors was Jerome, known for translating the Bible into Latin in the fourth century CE. At first, Jerome believed in the legitimacy of dreams, having had his own life-changing experience early on in his spiritual journey. But as time passed, he became increasingly concerned with the pagan practices around him and the potential for dreams to become a source of idolatry. As in Jeremiah's day (Jer. 23:25–32), he observed how some sought dream-visions for their own sake and showed little interest in following God. Tragically, Jerome's concerns led him to mistranslate two verses in the Old Testament, such that the instruction 'You shall not practise augury or *witchcraft*' became 'You should not practise augury nor *observe dreams*' (Lev. 19:26; Deut. 18:10).[3] This mistranslation had devastating consequences in the church for hundreds of years.

As we move into the sixth century and the period known as the Middle Ages, we see growing negativity towards dreams and visions. Another leading figure, Gregory the Great – the so-called 'teacher of the Middle Ages' – became wary and suspicious of dreams. Although he still believed in their validity and included several testimonies in his writings, he also warned against them by drawing on the verses in Leviticus from Jerome's Bible translation. According to Gregory, we should be careful to trust dreams because you can't tell where they come from.[4] Contemporary writer Morton Kelsey concludes that Gregory was 'torn between two attitudes and experiences' and 'he passed on the same split' to the church.[5] Gregory's writings led to increasing scepticism towards dream-visions for the next six centuries.

By the thirteenth century, reticence towards dream-visions was firmed up by another influential scholar and theologian, Thomas Aquinas. Although Aquinas was deemed one of the most brilliant thinkers of all time, his work was deeply influenced by Aristotle, the Greek philosopher who warned that dreams were dangerous and rarely connect us with God. Even though Aquinas experienced a life-changing vision towards the end of his life, his earlier writings came to influence thinking in western Europe in the fourteenth century and the years to follow.

In spite of the negativity towards dream-visions from the fourth century onwards, stories of God speaking in visual encounters persisted. Still, the problems of the past remained, continuing into the next two significant shifts in history – the Protestant Reformation and the Enlightenment.

A Historic Turnaround

In the early sixteenth century, a German monk named Martin Luther sparked off a protest that reverberated through the global church. This was a time when the Catholic Church was profoundly corrupted by power, greed and moral laxity, and Luther's ardent protests were well overdue. Even though Luther's spiritual journey was more about grace and faith than hearing God's voice, his work inflicted significant collateral damage on the validity of Spirit experiences for those who came after.

For Luther and his fellow Reformers, extrabiblical visionary experiences posed questions about divine authority and the source of revelation. Luther's own revelations pitted him against the established teachings of the Catholic Church, so the question became: how do you know who is right? Luther claimed the authority of Scripture, while the Catholic Church claimed the authority of the Church which allowed for God's voice to be heard in its midst. In the battle for truth, Spirit revelation got lost in the mix. Luther and fellow Reformers such as John Calvin dismissed the value of extrabiblical God-conversations for the sake of the Reformed cause.[6]

The Reformers' rejection of God-conversations outside Scripture left us with a legacy that persists in Protestant branches of the global church today.[7] In many places, Christians still believe that God doesn't speak apart from the Bible and certainly not in dream-visions. The debates over authority and doctrine during the Reformation meant that when it came to the dream-visions experienced by characters in Scripture, many concluded they were good for *them*, but not for *us*.

Enlightened?

A further turning point in the history of dream-visions came during the seventeenth and eighteenth centuries in the movement known as the Enlightenment. This was a time when human ingenuity and intellectualism flourished. From science and philosophy to the arts and music, humanity began to appreciate its true potential.

The Enlightenment gave us many great things: the scientific method, Newtonian physics, freedom of speech, and Mozart, to name a few. Our eyes were opened to the fact that the earth was not the centre of the universe, slavery was morally abhorrent in the light of human equality, and machines like the microscope could save our health. But among all the discoveries of the newly enlightened world, experts claimed that God was probably not real – or if he was, he wasn't that interested in us.

When a Dream Is Not a Dream

Philosophers drew heavily on the works of Aristotle who said that information could only be received through the natural senses and reason. If it couldn't be explained rationally, it probably wasn't true. If it couldn't be proven scientifically, it probably wasn't real.

Tragically, this type of rationalistic thinking permeated the church of the West. It damaged our faith in the supernatural, miracles and God-speech. We began to rationalize the stories of Jesus and the church, saying that miracles were only metaphors and that the gifts of the Spirit were no longer necessary since we now had the Bible.

It shouldn't be surprising that against this backdrop, dream-visions further lost their place at the centre of Christian experience. Translators even cut out all the references to dream-visions in the commentaries of the early church fathers![8] Modern rationalism shaped the church's thinking more than the example of the early church in Scripture. As our human 'enlightenment' grew, the Spirit's light diminished. As it's been said, dreams became God's 'forgotten language'.[9]

Enter the Pentecostals and Charismatics

In more recent times, some parts of the church have broken free of the faithless systems of Enlightenment thinking. We have realized that even with the insights of scientific rationalism, God can still speak, heal and intervene. Thanks largely to the fast-growing Pentecostal and Charismatic movements of the twentieth century, many of these truths have been restored to the church. We have learned that the work of the Spirit didn't die after all, that miracles still happen and God still has something to say.

Yet oddly, Pentecostal and Charismatic churches – again in the West – have yet to fully embrace the experience of God-dreams. We've received the first part of the promise in Acts 2:17: 'Your sons and daughters will prophesy', but we remain reticent about the second: 'your young men will see visions, your old men will dream dreams'. Charismatic and Pentecostal churches typically welcome prophecy and prophetic ministry, while rejecting dreams and visions.[10] Perhaps we are still reeling from Enlightenment thinking and the fear of getting it wrong. Tragically, many well-respected teachers and leaders today label dreams and visions by their very nature 'strange', 'unstable' and 'unreliable'. It has even been said that those who attend to them are 'less spiritual' than those who don't.[11]

Thankfully not everyone in the global church today shares this belief. The non-western, majority world has never stopped believing in the divine potential of dream-visions. In places where there is no western influence, people still view dreams as a primary medium through which spiritual powers speak. They haven't deviated from the testimony of Scripture, which demonstrates that even while dream-visions can appear strange at first, they may carry a message that changes the world.

Our Great Blind Spot

The first time I began studying the dream-visions of Scripture, I was shocked at their prevalence. My next question was: *How did I not see this before?* The place of dream-visions in the Bible has become an enormous blind spot in the church of today – a darkened shadow in the deep recesses of our thinking. It's a circular problem. Our unbelief in the legitimacy of dream-visions means we don't receive them, and in not receiving them, our unbelief is reinforced.

Given that dream-vision experiences are so common in Scripture, what have we done with them? For the most part, we've made them into something they're not. Today we're more likely to equate them with the sanctified human imagination.

Take Peter's famous words on the Day of Pentecost when the Spirit was poured out on the church (Acts 2:16–17). Peter's explanation for the events was that they fulfilled the promise of the prophet Joel:

> Your sons and daughters will prophesy,
> > your young men will see visions,
> > your old men will dream dreams.
>
> *Acts 2:17, quoting Joel 2:28*

This moment in history represents a game-changing shift under the New Covenant. Where once only the designated prophets could hear God's voice in dreams and visions and prophesy, now everyone could! Yet this understanding is rarely expressed in the contemporary Pentecostal-Charismatic church.[12] Instead, you might find any number of interpretations of Peter's sermon. One view proposes that we need to be older and more spiritually mature to interpret dreams, while visions are easier for the 'young' and spiritually immature to understand! Another says that since old men sleep more, they are prone to dreams that by their nature are fanciful and meaningless. 'Vision', on the other hand, points to destiny and purpose, so we must have vision while we're young! Since God enhances our ability to 'dream bigger', the message of Acts 2:16–17 becomes a call to youth to not waste their lives.[13]

Of course, having vision and purpose is a worthy goal, but it is *not* what Peter was saying.

In Peter's sermon, we are reminded that dreams and visions had always been the modus operandi of divine communication. They were Spirit-inspired experiences of revelation. They were neither fanciful nor meaningless and they certainly weren't personal plans and vision statements. Furthermore, the phrases 'sons and daughters' and 'young men and old men' are presented as an example of Hebrew parallelism. This is a *poetic device* (note how the words are arranged in most of our Bible translations) that emphasizes the *universality* of the Spirit's outpouring. The Spirit is now fully accessible to every demographic: young and old, male and female.

So, when Scripture speaks of Joseph having a dream that alluded to his future role as prime minister of Egypt (Gen. 37:5–11), it wasn't about 'thinking big'. Joseph laid his head on the pillow, fell asleep, and saw himself as a leader whose family would bow down to him, a dramatic reversal of the cultural norm. Similarly, when Scripture told of God's covenant relationship with Abraham (Gen. 15:7–20), it wasn't about having a godly plan for his life; and when it recounted an invitation to wisdom for Solomon, it wasn't about enhancing his leadership strategy (1 Kgs 3:5–15). Further, when Habakkuk was commanded to 'write the vision and make it plain', it wasn't about recording his ten-year plan. Joseph, Abraham and Solomon all literally fell asleep and had a dream. Habakkuk experienced scenes in his mind as he watched. God's voice came to all of them in picture language. They responded to the message, and their lives and those of many others were transformed as a result.

Our tendency to render dreams and visions a digestive problem, marginalize them as weird, or allegorize them as an expression of human ambition, reflects a legacy that betrays a lack of belief in God's ability to communicate today as he has done before. Our reluctance is largely grounded in fear – fears that have been present since the time of the early church. Concerns about getting it wrong, undermining the authority of the Bible, and embracing the supernatural, have all had their role in our rejection of dream-visions as a legitimate form of divine conversation today.

These fears are not irresolvable, however. It is possible to discern God's voice clearly in dream-visions, maintain the authority of the Bible (see my book, *The Church Who Hears God's Voice*), embrace the supernatural and honour human rationality! The question is: do we believe that God hasn't changed since the time his Spirit was first poured out on the church?

* * *

While not everyone understood the reasons behind my relocation from Melbourne to Sydney and the unusual God-dreams that directed it, they eventually proved themselves sound.[14] In the months leading up to their fulfilment, I found refuge in the testimonies of the biblical saints who saw God's faithfulness outworked in their own dream-visions. My faith was based on the promise of Jesus who sent his Spirit to speak to me in the same way that he spoke to the biblical characters. The result was that I experienced the wonder of God at work in the same powerful ways.

God's methods haven't changed. The testimonies of all the dreamers before us – in both Scripture and church history – reveal God's heartfelt desire to communicate by visionary means. The prophets experienced God-dreams; the Israelites experienced them; the disciples and early church leaders experienced them. Now it is time for us to experience them. If we truly believe the Spirit was given to the church under the New Covenant, we must embrace God's most powerful form of communication. It is simply a matter of faith.

Where Do Dreams Come From?

The Devil in the Mirror

One night Bronwyn had a dream that changed her life. In the dream, Bronwyn was in the master bedroom with her husband. She was trying to look in the mirror, but for some reason, her husband wouldn't allow her. He kept standing in front of her and pushing her aside. Eventually, she managed to look into the mirror. As she did, her husband's face morphed into the figure of a devil with bright red horns and ghoulish eyes. She woke up terrified.

Bronwyn's dream troubled her so much she began investigating her husband's bank accounts to see if there was anything amiss. Indeed, there was. Bronwyn's husband was cheating, not only on her, but on his friends and colleagues as well. He was later charged with fraud and sent to prison.

Thanks to a dream, Bronwyn escaped a dangerous situation. But where did the dream come from? Was it from God, giving her supernatural insight into her situation? Was it from an evil source trying to frighten her? Or did it come from within herself – perhaps revealing a truth that she had intuitively known but was unwilling to acknowledge?

Where do our dreams come from? This is an important question, since knowing the source of our dreams will determine our response to them.

In this chapter, we look at the *source* of our dreams. Dreams arise from three possible places:

1. Ourselves (natural dreams)
2. Other spirits (spirit dreams)
3. The voice of God (God-dreams).

We start with natural dreams.

1. Natural Dreams: Reflections of Ourselves

Natural dreams are those which arise from within ourselves. As our body rests, our minds get busy, processing the events and concerns of the day. As the writer of Ecclesiastes observed: 'A dream comes when there are many cares' (Eccl. 5:3).

Natural dreams constitute the vast majority of our dreams. They are most easily recognized by how they reflect the current happenings of our lives. The worries and cares of our day-to-day activities take on theatrical form as we sleep. For example, if you're angry with your boss at work, you may see yourself fighting him in a boxing ring in your dreams. If you're overwhelmed by your finances, you may see yourself drowning under a tidal wave. Or if you're longing for a red Ferrari, you may find yourself dreaming of one.

Where Do Dreams Come From?

Even though natural dreams are a product of our minds and not the direct voice of God, it doesn't mean they're of no value. As we've seen, natural dreams speak largely about *us*. They open up a window into our emotional lives and tell us what is going on beneath the surface (Chapter 2). When we understand them, they can become a powerful aid to our personal growth.

In one of my dreams, an old friend appeared. She lifted my shirt, cut open my abdomen and pulled out my intestines! There I stood with my guts hanging out, frantically trying to cover them up under my clothes! When it became obvious that I couldn't, I turned to others around me: 'Could you please help me put my guts back in?' Oddly, I woke up with stomach cramps.

At the time, I had experienced a hurtful betrayal by a friend. My 'guts' had effectively been 'ripped out', leaving me with a gaping wound! The dream highlighted my need for emotional healing even when I wasn't aware of it. It exposed a part of myself that had been covered up and hidden away. Afterwards, the dream prompted me to seek healing with the help of those I trusted.

In all the busyness of our lives, we are often unaware of what is going on in the hidden parts of ourselves. We put the masks on, 'keep calm and carry on', pretending everything's okay. Carl Jung described the hidden persona of our dreams as a 'shadow' and encouraged us to face our shadow self, confronting as that might be. In his words: 'In each of us there is another whom we do not know. He speaks to us in dreams and tells us how differently he sees us from the way we see ourselves.'[1]

The benefit of learning from our natural dreams is that they are largely unaffected by our own agendas. When we sleep, our conscious mind gets out of the way. American Episcopalian priest and dream therapist Morton Kelsey shows how a dream operates autonomously: 'The dream chooses its own time to speak, and we are not asked what topics will be brought up or what they will mean to us, or even what objects will be chosen to represent its meaning, for consciousness does not make the rules.'[2] In this way, dreams present an honest concept of who we are. We become aware of our fears, insecurities and desires. The reality confronts us in our sleep, even when we might resist it in our waking life.

This is the value of natural dreams. They offer us a way to face our inner selves and move forward with them. They cry out, 'Alert, alert! Something needs attention!'

How to respond to natural dreams

So how do we respond to natural dreams? We need to *work with them* in our journey of personal and spiritual growth. This is why counsellors are often trained in dreamwork, and why learning from our dreams has been described as having our own therapist!

Natural dreams have a way of pointing us towards wholeness and flourishing. Psychologists describe this move as an *integration* of the hidden self (the 'shadow') with the waking self. When we attend to the shadow, we can take the necessary steps to become the person we were formed to be. Even those who may not know God directly or profess a relationship with Jesus will experience this movement towards restoration and integration.

A young man once told me about his dream. He had repeatedly dreamt of finding a toad in his bed. In shock and repulsion, he would jump out of his bed and run into the closet. Then he would wake up. The man thought his dream was rather comical – until I asked him how his sex life was! His dream was saying it was time to stop hiding from the problem of intimacy in his marriage and deal with it. While it was unlikely to be the direct voice of God, it presented an opportunity to move towards restoration and freedom.

The call towards wholeness in our dreams shouldn't surprise us. If we are truly made in God's image as Scripture describes (Gen. 1:26–28), then we all have the capacity to emulate God's nature. We are all designed to reflect God's glory. That includes every part of our being: physical, mental and emotional.

This pull towards emotional health is reflected in our physical bodies. Each of us is built with an efficient and automated healing system. When we fall and injure ourselves, our bodies kick into action. Within moments, a message is sent to the brain as an alert to the immune system. Blood vessels tighten, platelets congregate, and scar tissue begins to form around the wound. Our body works to *heal itself*.

So, it seems, does the brain. Just as the body has inbuilt healing mechanisms to restore itself, so too does the mind. Sleep and dreaming are a God-given means to bring us into a place of mental health. Research has even demonstrated that stress transmitters in our brain are vastly reduced during REM sleep, suggesting that dreaming can reduce the trauma of painful experiences and provide psychological healing.[3] Dreaming has even been shown to reduce depression![4]

When we understand that God created the human psyche, we see the therapeutic value of natural dreams. There is no conflict between spirituality and psychology. In the dream, spiritual issues such as moral development, sin and relating to God meet with psychological issues such as sexuality, personality and personal relationships. So, too, the healing work of a spiritual director and therapist complement each other.[5] As Episcopalian minister and dream analyst John Sanford writes: 'The problem of the shadow demands both psychological insight and spiritual perspective if it is to be solved. At the level of the dream, psychology and religion are inseparable.'[6] Working with both helps make us complete.

Amber's night attacks

Amber was a young woman seeking to serve God wholeheartedly when she first told me about her dreams. In life, she is mild-mannered, sweet-natured and kind, but in her dreams she was crazed, angry and violent. The dreams regularly pictured her in the bedroom of her childhood home, fending off family members as they attacked her with knives and foul abuse. In one instance, her father even tried to rape her mother. The dreams weren't isolated – themes of aggression and violence occurred repeatedly over the years. Each time, she would wake up trembling in a sweat.

Amber had never spent time in gangs or playing with knives. She didn't grow up with physical abuse, nor was she given to swearing crudely. As she tells it, her childhood was normal and uneventful. Her aggressive dreams appeared to be so far from reality that she was prone to dismiss them.

Yet if we are to understand their psychological dynamic, Amber's dreams presented a truth that cried out to be heard. Something

Where Do Dreams Come From?

painful and unresolved lay buried beneath her calm and pleasant demeanour. This was the 'shadow self' spoken of by Jung. Amber's violent dreams were calling her to integrate who she was on the inside with who she was on the outside. She may not have seen it in her waking life, but it surfaced at night to remind her it was there. Though she didn't know it, the dissonance was affecting her.

After sharing her dreams with me, I suggested Amber see a counsellor. As she did, it became clear that she had been impacted by experiences in her childhood where misspoken words had pierced like daggers into her sensitive soul. With exaggerated flair, the dreams had revealed the unhealed parts of herself. In time and with the help of the counsellor, she cried, forgave her family members and healed the unspoken wounds that she had carried all her life. Today, those violent dreams have largely disappeared.

Amber's story reveals the importance of paying attention to our natural dreams, particularly those with recurring themes. They are a God-given mechanism to guide us towards healing and restoration. If we take time to consider their meaning and seek insight in counsel with others, we will learn from the message they carry. When experiencing a natural dream that feels significant or stands out in some way, ask questions such as: What is the common theme? What are you afraid of? Under attack from? Are you being chased? Lost something you can never find? Are you in danger?

Natural dreams are a God-given gift, sending us messages that can reveal deep-seated beliefs or wounds that hold us back. When we actively work with them, we will experience the freedom God has for us.

2. Spirit Dreams: Messages from Other Spirits

A second source of dream-visions is other spirits. As we've seen (Chapter 2), the vast majority of peoples around the world understand dreams to be a doorway between the natural and spiritual realms and a vehicle through which the spirits can communicate. The Native Americans have their dreamcatchers, the Chinese their dream books, and the Ancient Babylonians their professional dream interpreters. This view of spirit dreams also features in the sacred books of all the major religions – the Hindu Upanishads, the Buddhist Tripitaka, the Muslim Qur'an, the Jewish Torah and the Christian New Testament.

A Christian perspective on spirit dreams understands *other spirits* to include angelic beings, the spirits of those who have passed and evil spirits.

To begin with, angels in dream-visions are common in Scripture. Typically, the angel acts as God's messenger, as in the case of Zechariah's vision (Zech. 4), the story of Cornelius and Peter (Acts 10:2–26) and Paul's near shipwreck (Acts 27:23).

Spirits of the dead

The spirits of the dead may also appear in dream-visions. This is particularly common among Christians of the Global South[7] where the dead are deeply revered.[8] One theologian suggests that the appearance of those who have passed reflects the idea of the 'communion of the saints' (mentioned in the Apostles' Creed), in which the *whole* Body of Christ (both the living and the dead) celebrates God's goodness in our memories and in the future.[9] After all, we know that through Jesus' death and resurrection, the dead who were 'imprisoned' were 'made alive' in Christ (1 Pet. 3:19; 4:6).[10]

In Scripture, the spirits of the dead appear in the vision of Moses and Elijah at Jesus' transfiguration (Matt. 17:1–8) and in John's visions at the time of the early church (Revelation). In John's case, twenty-four elders from every 'tribe and language and people and nation' appear, with one of them speaking to encourage John (Rev. 5:8–10). Later, the spirits of those who have been martyred cry out for justice (Rev. 6:9–11). In both cases, the spirits who have passed speak to encourage the living in their faith, bringing messages that are consistent with the heart of God. They act as a 'cloud of witnesses', cheering on the church to run their race with perseverance (Heb. 12:1).

This 'cloud of witnesses' is also seen in a contemporary dream coming from the slums of Kampala, Uganda. Mama Agnes was living there with her husband and 1-year-old daughter Agnes when she became pregnant with her second child. Tragically, shortly after giving birth to a boy, her daughter Agnes died. As a result, Mama Agnes fell into a deep depression, and wanted to die to be with her daughter. Then, things got worse. Her husband lost his job, their landlord threw them out, and they found themselves homeless on the streets.

One day not long after, Mama Agnes heard music coming from the nearby church and felt compelled to join the service. She stayed all day until evening. That night, she had a dream. In the dream, she saw her daughter dressed in white and holding a Bible. She was surrounded by others, also dressed in white. Then her daughter spoke to her. She told her mother how happy she was and that she should take heart and not worry because she was with Jesus. Even though things were hard, she should stop grieving and follow Jesus. Also, Jesus would give her another baby girl.

The next day, Agnes gave her life to Jesus.

A few days later, Agnes shared her story with her husband, who had been away in search of work. To her surprise, he'd had a dream too – the same one! Afterwards, Agnes' husband joined with her in deciding to follow Jesus. A few months passed, and Mama Agnes became pregnant with a baby girl.[11]

Evil spirits

However, not all spirit appearances in dream-visions reflect the heart of God. Evil spirits may also appear. Jesus explicitly taught that we have an enemy who comes to steal, kill and destroy (John 10:10). He regularly encountered evil spirits in his waking life and taught his disciples to have authority over them (Mark 3:14–15). Early church teachings also reinforce the activity of spiritual agents that work to oppose God's kingdom (e.g. 1 Pet. 5:8).

Dreams from evil spirits can be traumatizing. In Scripture, Job's friend Eliphaz describes his own experience: 'fear and trembling seized me and made all my bones shake. A spirit glided past my face, and the hair on my body stood on end' (Job 4:14–15). Professor of neurology and psychiatry Patrick McNamara, who has researched the appearance of supernatural creatures in dreams, extensively reports that dreams of monsters, demons, spirits and unusual animals often attack or target the dreamer in some way. The dreams are characterized by fear, confusion and a sense of powerlessness, and are always malevolent.[12]

Just as Holy Spirit has easy access to us while we sleep, so too does the enemy of our souls. As we may be more open to God's voice when our conscious minds are switched off, so too we may be vulnerable to the forces of darkness as we sleep. Cultural anthropologist Charles Kraft suggests that the Enemy likes to attack when 'our resistance is down'.[13] McNamara's research further affirms this clinically, with most cases of involuntary spirit-influence occurring overnight.[14]

We also know that dreams involving evil spirits may contain supernatural insight and premonitions. After all, they are accessing the spiritual realm. Even the Scriptures acknowledge the power of other spirits to 'get it right' (see Deut. 13:1–3; Acts 16:16). However, just because demonic dreams contain supernatural knowledge doesn't mean they should be listened to. Those who follow Jesus are called to listen to God's voice alone.

King Saul learned the importance of this lesson in the early days of Ancient Israel (1 Sam. 28). At the time, the Philistine army was threatening to attack, and Saul was desperate to hear from God. Previous decisions had distanced him from God, and he couldn't hear God's voice in the normal way through dream-visions and prophets (v. 6). So he consulted a witch, even while knowing it was forbidden. As a result, the witch called up the spirit of the prophet Samuel to deliver a message.

It's an unusual tale and theologians debate its place in Saul's story. For the sake of this discussion, the story acts as a warning against seeking guidance from spirits other than God. The Israelites of Saul's time were forbidden to engage in divination, pagan worship[15] and dream-visions arising from other sources.[16] Even though Saul had received accurate information, he was wrong to seek it from spirits other than God. As the writer of Isaiah asked: 'When someone tells you to consult mediums and spiritists, who whisper and mutter, should not a people enquire of their God? Why consult the dead on behalf of the living?' (Isa. 8:19).

The Holy Spirit was sent to us so that we may go directly to God for guidance. If we look to other sources, we may find ourselves hearing from evil spirits in our dreams. Like Saul, we may be opening ourselves up to deception at a time when we are most vulnerable – at night.

How to respond to spirit dreams

We know that we shouldn't consult sources other than God, but sometimes spirit dreams seem to arise apart from our own bidding. How do we respond then?

If the spirit is an angel acting as God's messenger, we should heed them as one sent from God. Cornelius demonstrated this response when he followed the angel's instructions to send his servants to Peter (Acts 10:22). Similarly, the apostle Paul responded in faith after the angel spoke to him about the shipwreck (Acts 27:21–26).

The same posture applies to our response to the spirits of those who have passed – but only when they communicate in line with

Where Do Dreams Come From?

the nature and character of Jesus. Like John in his visions of the martyrs, we can welcome their comfort and encouragement.

Of course, the same is not true of dream encounters that involve the presence of an evil spirit. In these cases, our response should be to actively resist them. Part of this process involves asking *why* the evil spirit has come. Demonic dreams have several possible causes. For Charles Kraft, harassment may be brought on by 'garbage' in a person,[17] such as fear, guilt, anger and lust. Curses and vows may also be at work. Another common issue is past or present involvement in occultic practices such as séances, witchcraft, and with occultic items and objects.[18] Past trauma or abuse may also be at play.[19]

Finally, our own sinful choices may have opened the door to demonic influence in our dream-visions. Respected Catholic healer Neal Lozano describes it this way: 'The spirit is no fouler than the sin it hides behind. The sin we have accommodated, the thought pattern that offends the One who made us, the despair we carry and have grown used to, the lust we secretly feed, the unforgiveness and bitterness we nurse – these are the expressions of the influence of evil spirits.'[20] And so when contemplating an evil presence in our dreams, we should ask: How is my relationship with God? Is there any place I have allowed the Enemy to enter my life? Is there sin I am harbouring that I need to repent of?

Because the reasons for dreams of evil spirits are spiritual, it makes sense that our response to them is also spiritual. These are not experiences to be feared, but areas to be confronted with the authority made available through Jesus (Matt. 28:18). In Christ, we have victory over the demonic realm. Our response therefore should include repentance, prayer and submission to the Holy Spirit. It may also involve practical steps to deal with the root of the problem. As we 'submit' ourselves to God and 'resist the devil', he will 'flee' from us (Jas 4:7).

The power of God at work as we sleep is vividly demonstrated in the testimony of a pastor who works with First Nations peoples of Australia. Simone tells of how in the course of her ministry, she met a witchdoctor. The witchdoctor told her that a spirit was going to visit her at night. 'No!' Simone declared. 'You can't touch my dreams – I'm protected by Jesus.'

That night, Simone had a dream in which she saw her entire body as a door. In the dream, she heard someone knocking on it. Immediately, she knew it was the spirit sent by the witchdoctor. She also knew that it couldn't enter without permission. The spirit couldn't talk to her or visit her because Jesus kept her safe.

In another case, a man woke up with the impression that claws were digging into his face. The pain in his eyes and mouth was physical and kept him from speaking out loud. So he began calling on the name of Jesus in his mind. Once he rebuked the demon, sleep returned. Upon waking, he discovered that the owners of the house where he was staying kept a large collection of tribal objects. The next day they were quickly removed.[21] Just as the Ephesians who practised sorcery destroyed their scrolls and repented in Paul's day (Acts 19:13–20), our response to evil spirits may also require practical steps.

Through Jesus, we always have the power over sin, evil and the demonic. Just as we can resist evil spirits when we're awake, we can resist them when we sleep.

What about nightmares?

If you have ever had a nightmare, you will know the profound sense of relief when you wake to realize it was a dream. Nightmares are characterized by extreme fear, terror and dread, made all the more terrifying as they feel so real. Psychologists define nightmares as 'lengthy, elaborate dreams with imagery that evokes fear, anxiety, or sadness. The dreamer may wake up to avoid the perceived danger.'[22] In many cases, nightmares lead to sleep disorders and difficulties returning to sleep. They are particularly common among children and young adolescents.

Some nightmares come from the direct activity of evil spirits, in which case we need to pray against them. However, not all bad dreams are spiritual. A nightmare may also be a natural dream. Psychologists and spiritual directors Louis M. Savary, Patricia H. Berne and Strephon Kaplan Williams describe nightmares as an 'incomplete' dream.[23] They explain how we wake up from them to escape the fear of being overwhelmed, but in doing so, experience only temporary solace. The dream remains *unresolved* and continues to plague us.

A good example of this lack of resolution in dreams is seen in the life of one of Savary, Berne and Williams' clients. Harold was a war veteran whose recurring dreams of bloodshed and death caused him so much trauma they impacted his physical health. Decades on from battle, he was still tormented by them. Though he had never spoken of his experiences in his waking life, the pain of his war years refused to be ignored as he slept.

In therapy with his counsellors, the man was invited to 'complete the nightmare' rather than escape it.[24] With their guidance and prayer, the man revisited his dreams and was able to work through his feelings of helplessness and grief. The whole process allowed him to reconcile his faith in God with the horrors he had experienced in the midst of war.

This process can also be applied to children. The nightmare becomes a springboard to conversation. Perhaps the monster chasing them in their dream is a bully at school they feel helpless to respond to. Or the cliff they're falling from is a sense of failure in a task they're struggling to master. Nightmares can then offer a pathway to resolution.

As a form of natural dream, nightmares call us to actively work with their content rather than just ignore them or pray them away. Resolution may involve releasing our anger, pain or fear. It may require revisiting memories that are ugly and traumatic. But careful dreamwork offers a way for negative experiences to be changed into something positive.

3. God Dreams: Jesus' Continuing Voice

The final source of our dream-visions is God. Throughout biblical history, dream-visions were God's modus operandi, first in the lives of the Old Covenant prophets, then in the life of Jesus and, after Pentecost, in the lives of the early Christians.

Scripture shows us that at first it was largely the prophets who experienced God-dreams. They were God's appointed mouthpieces, specially chosen and trained to deliver God's messages to his people. Their visionary experiences were clearly supernatural, offering glimpses of the future and sometimes impacting the dreamer physically. The prophets' dreams were viewed as legitimate and authoritative, shaping the decisions of kings and priests and calling the people to live according to God's ways.

There was a downside to this arrangement, however. God-dreams were largely limited to the experts, such that you had to go through a prophet to hear God's voice. Even the prophets knew that this set-up was not ideal. They looked forward to a *better* time – a time when God's Spirit would come on *all* people – when not only the Moseses, Jeremiahs and Ezekiels of the day would hear from God in dream-visions, but everyone would be prophetic just like them (Num. 11:29). Instead of God's words being 'written on tablets of stone' by others, they would be spoken to people's hearts (see Ezek. 36:26; Jer. 31:34). No longer would they need a neighbour to teach them because they would all know God for themselves (Jer. 31:34). This arrangement would be a *new* covenant – a fully upgraded version of their own experience. The prophets spoke of it, waited and longed for it, praying and hoping they would get to see it.

Then on that monumental Day of Pentecost, it happened . . . Peter was the first to recognize it: *Now everyone can hear from God through dreams and visions! Everyone can now prophesy!* (Acts 2:16–17). But the promise was not only for those assembled in Jerusalem that day. It was for their children and for their children and for every generation to come (Acts 2:39). The promise is for us! God speaks in dream-visions today. And just as they did in ancient times, God-dreams have a very particular purpose.

Not just a dream

During the 2000s, there was an award-winning American TV show called *Medium*. The star of the show was a suburban mum named Allison DuBois who had a special gifting. Amid the bustle of family life, Allison would receive supernatural messages in dreams. She would then use them to work with law enforcement to solve crimes.

The series was always entertaining, each episode ending with a cliffhanger and a creative twist. But somehow you could always tell the stories were written by a scriptwriter. The plotlines were clever, but not quite clever enough. They bore just enough hints to solve the crime, but you could always tell there was a human inspiring them.

God-dreams can provide solutions too. They can also contain otherworldly thoughts and glimpses of foreknowledge that extend beyond human reach. But the main difference between Allison DuBois's dreams and God-dreams is their overarching *purpose*. God-dreams have a *personal* agenda. They are designed to build relationship. God-dreams reveal the One who speaks personally and intimately. We get to know the God behind the message. When it's a God-dream, we will see him more. We will be transformed by his love. We will be led into worship.

The ability to *know* God through dream-visions is made more pertinent because Jesus has come. Not only can we hear from God in the same way as the Old Covenant prophets; we also have a clearer framework for who God is. This is part of the reason why hearing God under the New Covenant is superior to hearing him under the Old (2 Cor. 3:7–18; Heb. 8:6–11). The incarnation, death and resurrection of Jesus make everything clearer.

When Jesus was on earth, he told his disciples what the Spirit would talk about when he had gone. The Spirit would first *remind* them of the truths he had established when he was with them (John 14:26) (now recorded for us as the Scriptures). But because Jesus had more to say, the Spirit would also speak about what was 'yet to come' (John 16:13). In other words, the Spirit would speak to apply the gospel wherever the disciples went (John 16:12). It would be better than having the living, breathing Jesus in their midst (John 16:7)!

As it was for the early disciples, so it is for us. When God speaks in dream-visions today, it comes as Jesus' continuing voice. The Spirit speaks to remind us of the truths Jesus established and then applies them to our lives. This means that the message of God-dreams will always be consistent with the life and person of Jesus.

How to respond to God-dreams

When we understand God-dreams to be Jesus' continuing voice, we know how to respond to them. God-dreams lead us to follow Jesus. As clever and powerful as they may be, we must never overlook the person for the spectacle. They are part of an ongoing *relationship* that calls for submission and active participation.

When Jesus was on earth, he called his disciples to follow (John 10:27). He didn't need to speak in dreams and visions because everything he said and did was a revelation of God's nature and character. He was the perfect image of the invisible God, the 'living Word' of God in the flesh. But this revelation was futile without a response. Acting on the revelation of Jesus was what brought change to the disciples' lives.

The same principle applies today. When Holy Spirit speaks in dream-visions, we are called to follow. Once the message has been tested and discerned to be genuine, we respond in faith, believing what God has said. As we do, our relationship with God will deepen, our hearts will be transformed and God's mission will come to pass in our lives.

Nikki is a pastor at a regional Australian church who has witnessed this process in her own life. In a dream, she saw herself preaching at a women's conference at the church pastored by her friend Louise. After her sermon, Nikki asked the mothers to stand with their babies as a prophetic declaration on behalf of the infertile women in the room. As she did, something profoundly supernatural took place and healing came to many. Then she woke up.

A few weeks later, Nikki told Louise about the dream. To her surprise, she learned that infertility had been a pressing issue at Louise's church and Louise had been interceding intensely about it at that time.

Listening to Nikki share her dream, Louise sensed the presence of the Holy Spirit, and decided to put the dream into action. She invited Nikki to preach at her upcoming women's conference. There, Nikki enacted the dream as she had seen it. She asked all the mothers in the room to stand in faith for those who were infertile. Together they prayed and believed God for healing.

Soon after the conference, Nikki received a text from a friend who had been struggling with infertility for many years. The message was a photo of a newly conceived foetus from an ultrasound! Ten months later, five babies had been born in Louise's

Where Do Dreams Come From?

congregation with another five on the way. Louise tells how one new father cried his eyes out the whole way through the baby dedication. He and his wife had been waiting for a child for ten years! Their miracle came because two women recognized the voice of God in a dream and acted in faith on what they'd heard.

* * *

While we know that dreams arise from three different sources, it isn't always easy to discern them. Sometimes God-dreams are clear; other times they're not. They can even be a bit of a mix – a God-moment in the midst of a natural scene. Often, they come in broken fragments or just a glimpse of an image that passes by.

Since most of our dreams are natural, it's generally wise to start with that assumption. God-dreams are less common than natural dreams and require a careful testing process (see Chapter 12). Many of our dreams are not even worth remembering!

In short, when dreams come from ourselves, we need to work with them. When dreams come from evil spirits, we need to pray against them. When they come from God, we should follow them.

PART II

HOW TO UNDERSTAND YOUR DREAM-VISIONS

Anatomy of a Dream

A Lost Load of Corpses

I am not a fan of horror movies, but one of the more significant God-dreams in my life seemed to come straight out of one.

In the dream, I was driving along a highway when I hit a traffic jam. Banked up in front of me was a long line of cars stretching endlessly to the horizon. Frustrated, I got out of my car and started walking down the highway to find out what was wrong.

The reason for the traffic jam soon became clear. A hearse had lost its load of coffins! Worse still, the coffins had tipped over and four to five dead bodies now lay strewn across the road.

I watched from the side of the road as bystanders rushed to help. One by one they picked up the corpses, placed them back in their coffins and loaded them onto the hearse. Even though everyone was panicking, I felt strangely calm. I even started checking the bodies in case there was any life left in them. There wasn't. Their eyes stared at me blankly and their skin was pasty and cold.

One corpse in particular stood out. It was a young woman with a mass of long red curly hair. Her hair was pinned behind her head by a large green enamel clip in the shape of a butterfly. I watched as a bystander picked her up, threw her over his shoulder and loaded her into the hearse. Then I woke up.

Afterwards, the bizarre scenes lingered in my mind. *Why was I dreaming of dead bodies?* I hadn't been watching movies with corpses or thinking about death. I hadn't attended a funeral that week. Where had it come from?

When I arrived at work that morning, I began telling my colleague about the dream. I was laughing as I told it – it seemed so bizarre. Then midway through the retelling, it suddenly became clear! I knew the dream had come from God and I knew exactly what it meant. In the ensuing months, it became a profound source of encouragement and peace.

But how could a dream about a lost load of corpses on a highway bring peace and encouragement? And how did I know it was from God?

At first glance, the dream makes little sense, but when you understand its 'anatomy' – its different elements and how they work together to communicate – the meaning becomes clear. The same is true of all our dream-visions.

In this chapter, we'll explore a framework for interpreting dream-visions using the example of my dream about the lost load of corpses. This framework can then be used to decipher the meaning of any visionary experience.

The God Dreams Framework

Dream-visions have an uncanny way of provoking questions. We find ourselves asking, 'What does it mean?'

The same was true for the biblical characters. For example, after one of the most important God-conversations in the early church – Peter's vision of an unappetizing lunch – Peter is seen walking around the house wondering about its meaning (Acts 10:17,19).

Zechariah too had questions about his vision at the time of Ancient Israel. Though some of the symbols were familiar to him – the olive trees and the seven-branched lampstand (Zech. 4:1–14) – the message wasn't immediately obvious. Afterwards, we see both the angel and Zechariah asking questions: 'Do you know what these are? "No, what are they?" What are the two olive trees on the right and the left of the lampstand? "What are the two olive branches beside the two gold pipes that pour out golden oil?" Do you not know what these are?' (adapted from Zech. 4). Question after question, back and forth they go. Zechariah had to ask a lot of questions before he finally understood what God was saying about the rebuilding of the temple.

The dream-vision experience engages us in a learning journey by provoking questions. In the search for understanding, our first step should not be to try to find ready answers in a dream dictionary. As Jesus taught, discovery is preceded by pursuit. We're called to a posture of asking, seeking and knocking (Matt. 7:7), motivated by a desire to become self-aware, discover our identity and find wholeness. Ultimately it is a search for God himself.

To that end, the God Dreams framework uses a series of questions to decipher the message of our dream-visions. All five are important:

> **THE GOD-DREAMS FRAMEWORK**
>
> **01 Setting**
> What is happening in my life?
>
> **02 Emotions**
> How did I feel in the dream?
>
> **03 Symbols**
> What do the symbols mean to me?
>
> **04 Source**
> Where did the dream come from?
>
> **05 Response**
> What is the dream asking me to do?

Using these questions, we can begin to understand the meaning of the dream with the lost load of corpses. We start with the *setting*.

01 Setting
What Is Happening in My Life?

The first and possibly the most important question relates to our setting: *What is happening in my life?*

Dreams come in the context of our current situation. They relate to how we are interacting with our circumstances at the time. If the dream is from God, the Spirit will be speaking to remind us of the foundations of our faith established by Jesus and how to apply it to our setting. If the dream comes from ourselves, it will reflect our current or past state, exposing issues and ideas that may be triggered by happenings around us. If it is from other spirits, it will be in response to our particular spiritual journey.

So, we ask, what has been happening in my life recently? What is on my mind? What questions am I asking, or issues am I facing? What hopes or desires am I carrying? What is of concern to me right now?

Without knowing the setting of our lives at the time of our visionary experiences, interpretation becomes an exercise in guesswork. I've shared my dream of the lost load of corpses in countless seminars around the world and asked the audience what they think it means. The answers have been as wide-ranging as they were creative. Some suggested the dream revealed a fear of death. Others said that the corpses might be people in my life who were going to die. Still others thought that I was frustrated by Sydney traffic or had an unhealthy obsession with zombie movies! Without an understanding of what was happening in my life, an outside observer will have little idea. Knowing the setting is key.

So, what was happening in my life at the time of the dream about the corpses?

At the time, I was facing a personal crisis. I had no permanent place to live, a promised job had fallen through, my finances were in trouble, and an important friendship had broken down. The corpses effectively represented the different areas of my life that had 'died'. At the time of the dream, my heart had been heavy with disappointment and, in spite of all my efforts, I couldn't change my circumstances. In fact, the night before, I had announced to God that I was quitting. I'd had enough! While I had no idea what that meant practically, my declaration marked a point of desperation and despair.

Perhaps now you can begin to see the significance of my dream. What did my decision to quit look like in the vision? What implications would it have on my life and what was the solution?

02 Emotions
How Did I Feel in the Dream?

The second question of the God Dreams framework asks: *How did I feel in the dream?* As we know, dreams can powerfully impact our emotions. We can wake up from a dream in a cold sweat of fear, riding high with joy or feeling overwhelmed with despair. It's as though we have lived the visions we've seen.

The emotional element of a dream-vision is part of the message. How you felt as the scenes play out will be an important key to interpretation. Did the dream leave you fearful? Excited? Peaceful? Motivated? Sad? Worried? Hopeful?

Also note if your emotions change significantly in the dream or if they seem out of place. Oddly, you may feel happy in a dream when the scene appears sad. Or you may feel sad when the scene is happy. The disparity is part of the message.

This is what I experienced in my dream about the corpses. It was a macabre scene, but I was strangely calm. Why did I feel so peaceful when surrounded by death? In the dream, my response had been pragmatic – checking the state of the corpses – even while everyone else was panicking. Noting my feelings clarifies the solution presented by the vision.

03 Symbols
What Do the Symbols Mean to Me?

The third question of our interpretative framework asks: *What do the symbols mean to me?* Because dream-visions typically speak a symbolic language, we need to identify the key images and explore what they mean. As we do, the message will become clearer.

Note how the question asks what the symbols mean to *you*. This is important. Two people can have the same dream with vastly different meanings. This is because symbols relate primarily to the dreamer's life. While there are a number of generic symbols that are common to different cultures and people groups, for the most part, symbols have a unique expression. They send a message that is tailored to the dreamer.

In my dream about the corpses, did you notice the key symbols? There were three. The first was the traffic jam on the highway. I'd been travelling along the road, but my journey had been stopped by the hearse's lost load. Can you now see the significance of the traffic jam? In my waking life, I'd announced to God the night before that I was quitting. I was no longer willing to hope for the future God had promised, because everything around me had fallen into a heap. The traffic jam symbolized the implications of my decision. It had brought my life journey to a halt.

The second symbol is the corpses – the four to five dead bodies strewn across the road. Knowing my circumstances, you can now see how the corpses represented the different areas of my life that had 'died'. My job, my finances, my prospects . . . all were gone. The dreams that I had carried in my heart were now lifeless and inert, leaving me with nothing to hope for. The dream reiterated the fact that my hopes had died and were on their way to the grave.

Finally, the third symbol – the young woman with the green butterfly clip in her hair. For some reason, she had stood out among the corpses. Perhaps now you can see why. She wore the symbol of a butterfly – that astounding creature that finds its full expression only after it 'dies' to the form of a caterpillar and metamorphoses into something new and beautiful.

04 Source
Where Did the Dream Come From?

The fourth question in the God Dreams framework relates to the source of our dreams: *Where did the dream come from?* As we know, dreams arise from three different places: ourselves, other spirits and God. Once we've discerned their source, we will know how to respond.

The process of discerning our dreams takes time and practice. It isn't always clear at first. In the case of my corpses dream, it was immediately apparent that the dream didn't come from me; one of the tell-tale signs of natural dreams is that they regurgitate the activities of our waking lives and, in particular, our *recent* waking lives. While this dream accurately reflected my circumstances, it also bore a kind of otherworldly wisdom that offered an *alternative* way of looking at them.

Once I understood the meaning of the corpses dream, it became clear where it came from. The message was consistent with a God who keeps his promises and who could bring good out of loss and despair. It resonated with the God I had walked with in the past, and gave me hope for what was ahead. Though my faith had been fading, God's faithfulness had not.

There was also another tip-off. The evening after the dream, I was at home watching a movie. A key character in the film was a young woman with a mass of long red hair. In one scene, she turned around to reveal a green enamel hairclip pinning back her hair. It was in the shape of a butterfly!

I was so taken aback by what I had seen that I switched on the director's commentary. The director explained that the butterfly clip was placed on the woman's head intentionally to symbolize the changes that would take place in her life. Just as a caterpillar transforms into a butterfly, her life would be 'rebirthed' in a new way through the death of her current dreams. The director also explained how he chose to style the hairclip in bright green to represent the new life that would come. It was a subtle but powerful way to communicate hope in the face of despair.

05 Response
What Is the Dream Asking Me to Do?

The final question in our interpretative framework points to our response: *What is the dream asking me to do?* Whatever their source, dreams will always invite a response. There will be new ideas to ponder, insights to be reflected on and, usually in the case of God-dreams, actions to be taken. Transformation into the nature of Jesus lies at the heart of every God-conversation.

While the images of corpses in my dream affirmed the deadness of my hopes and desires, it also revealed what God was asking of me. My quitting attitude was causing a traffic jam! I had 'dropped' the promises of God for my life. Even though they were dead (there was little doubt about that), I needed to pick them up again, load them back into the vehicle of my heart and keep going. Only then could new life come.

No wonder the dream gave me hope once I understood it! This was surely the voice of the One who could resurrect any dead

Anatomy of a Dream

situation. My only response was to act in faith. Would I believe what God was saying?

The dream restored my confidence in God's promises. After recognizing its source, I made a decision to pick up my dead hopes and keep going. As I persevered in the days and months ahead, circumstances around me began to shift. My job was restored. I found a place to live. The promises of God unfolded beautifully in my workplace. But perhaps the greatest joy was seeing the butterfly emerge in my own heart.

* * *

Not every dream will have the same depth of clarity as the dream about the lost load of corpses. Most dreams are merely fragments of images and scenes linked together in an ad hoc fashion. But now and then, we will have a dream that impresses us deeply. It seems to contain wisdom and speaks from someone other than ourselves. It calls us to ask, 'What does it mean?'

The five questions of interpretation guide us to an answer. Why not try the framework on one of your own dreams? Clarity comes with practice. Work with a friend or family member, reflecting on your setting, the feelings and the symbols. Pray about what God may be showing you and carefully choose your response. As we practise interpretation, asking questions and seeking understanding, we will see the power and efficacy of the mysterious and wonderful language of imagery.

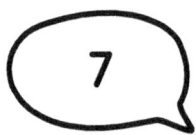

Peter's Vision of an Unappetizing Lunch

The apostle Peter was spending time in prayer while waiting for lunch one morning on the rooftop of his friend's home in Joppa. While he was praying, he fell into a trance and had a vision. He saw the heavens open, and a large tablecloth being lowered from above.

You can imagine what Peter was thinking: *Great! What's for lunch?* But when the cloth opened up, it revealed an unexpected menu. Laid out on the cloth was an array of reptiles, birds and four-footed creatures . . . For Jews of the first century like Peter, this was *unclean* or *non-kosher* food! Peter's stomach would have reeled at the spread.

Then, even more shockingly, a voice beamed down from the heavens: 'Get up, kill and eat!' Peter's response was defiant: 'No! I would never eat unclean food!'

Then the vision repeated itself. The cloth came down from heaven. *Great. What's for lunch?* The cloth opened up. *Oh no! Unclean animals.* The voice: 'Get up, kill and eat.'

Peter's Vision of an Unappetizing Lunch

Three times it happened. The cloth from heaven. The unclean food. And the voice: 'Get up, kill and eat.'

When Peter came to, he was troubled and confused. How could a voice be telling him to eat food that was expressly forbidden by the Jewish law? Yet the voice seemed to come from heaven. Could it be from God?

As he was pondering the vision, Peter heard a noise outside at the gate. He went downstairs to see who was there. But who did he see? *Ugh. Roman soldiers from Caesarea. Gentiles. Unclean!* Peter would have felt the same revulsion as with the non-kosher food. To make it worse, the visitors invited him to visit the home of their master, Cornelius! This was another prohibition in the Jewish law. Jews were not to socialize with Gentiles because they were *unclean*.

Now the vision made sense!

Peter's experience on the rooftop in Joppa is one of the best examples of a symbolic dream-vision in the life of the early church (Acts 10:1–23). It is probably the *most* significant in terms of its ramifications. This makes it an ideal model for us to learn from.

In this chapter, we apply the God Dreams framework to Peter's God-conversation to consider how he arrived at its meaning. We also unpack question four in more detail ('Where did the dream come from?') by looking at how Peter discerned his vision to be from God.

01 What Was Happening in Peter's Life?

The first question of dream-vision interpretation considers the setting: *What was happening in Peter's life at the time of his vision?*

We know that Peter was called by Jesus to play an important role in building the church (Matt. 16:18). For three years, he'd been prepared for the task. It had been a thorough and challenging process that required constant change and growth. The process was now complete. The man once known as *Simon*, meaning 'reed', was now named *Peter*, meaning 'rock'. Having experienced a radical transformation as a student of Jesus, and then the reception of the Holy Spirit at Pentecost, Peter was now ready to fulfil his call. Once a common fisherman, Peter was to become an apostle and pioneer of the greatest commission of all.

But the question was: how was he to do it? Jesus had left no specific instructions about what the church should look like and there were few models to draw from. The concept of 'church' was unprecedented! How should the church be set up? If 'church' in the original sense meant a 'gathering' of people for a common purpose, what should the disciples do when they met together? And perhaps most importantly, who should be invited to join them?

Up until that point, the only disciples Peter knew were Jews who had come to believe in Jesus as their long-awaited Messiah. Jesus himself was a Jew who followed the customs of his faith, visiting the synagogue, joining pilgrimages to Jerusalem and participating in the annual feasts. Jesus also explicitly said that his main earthly ministry was to his own people (Matt. 15:24). So it wouldn't be surprising that Peter would follow his master and focus entirely on them. Peter's travels around the country to this point had all been aimed at Jews – both those who had come to believe the good news and those who had not yet heard it. More recently, he'd been spending time in prayer at the home of his friend, Simon the Tanner. It's then that the vision comes...

How Did Peter Feel in the Dream?

The second question of our God Dreams framework focuses on the emotions. Our feelings are part of the message, so it's important to identify them. We also note any emotional changes that occur. So the question becomes: *How did Peter feel in the dream-vision?*

Here we need to step into Peter's reality. As a first-century Jew, Peter's very identity was shaped by a myriad of laws governing every aspect of his life. These had been handed down since the time of Moses and were religiously upheld by members of the Jewish community. Over 600 laws regulated the allocation of work and leisure time, religious rituals and social gatherings, hygiene practices and, of course, what they ate at mealtimes. At the heart of all these regulations was the notion of being separate from non-Jews – the so-called 'Gentiles'. This separation marked the Jews' identity and allegiance as God's chosen people.

It shouldn't be difficult, then, to imagine Peter's response to the culinary spread in his vision. Remembering that he had been schooled all his life to avoid foods such as these, his feelings would have been visceral, with the words of the Levitical law hammering in his mind: '*You must not eat* the meat of animals that chew the cud but do not have a divided hoof; they are unclean for you. *You must not eat* creatures of the sea without fins or scales. *You must not eat* certain types of flying insects, birds or animals that move along the ground . . .' (adapted from Lev. 11, italics mine).

Remember too that the vision came as Peter was *waiting for lunch*. He would have been hungry, perhaps salivating at the thought of the contents on the cloth. Then when he sees the spread, there can be little doubt of his revulsion. If you can picture yourself fronting up hungry for lunch and being offered a plate of innards and offal, you may get the idea.

Although the account doesn't explicitly describe Peter's feelings, we do know he was deeply impacted by what he saw. At first, he must have felt anticipation at the prospect of food. But his eagerness would have quickly dissipated with the command from heaven, turning into disgust, and then confusion.

We can further trace Peter's emotions in the dream-vision as the story unfolds. There was no coincidence in the timing of the Gentiles' arrival at the home where Peter was staying. It was *just as* Peter was wondering about the meaning of his vision that the visitors appeared at the gate. Unbeknown to him, God had been speaking to another man named Cornelius who lived two days' walk away in Caesarea. Cornelius was a Gentile, a 'God-fearer' – someone who was interested in the God of the Jews, but still an outsider. Through a vision of an angel, God had told Cornelius to send messengers to Joppa and invite Peter back to his home. It was this second God-conversation that brought the Gentiles to Peter.

How would Peter have felt when he saw the visitors at the gate? Like the food in his vision, Gentiles were ritually *unclean* and Jews were forbidden to associate with them. This included *all* settings: social, work-related and religious. Like many laws in Judaism, the rationale was to keep the people separate and wholly consecrated to God. To associate with Gentiles was to invite the prospect of idolatry, a contravention of the first commandment. As a devout Jew, the idea of visiting the Gentiles' home would have been as sickening as eating shellfish or an animal without a divided hoof. Every emotion in Peter's body would have told him to slam the door in their face.

What Did the Symbols Mean to Peter?

Now we turn to the third question of our interpretative framework: *What did the symbols mean to Peter?*

There are two key symbols in Peter's vision. The first is the unclean food. Sometimes people conclude that the vision was about dietary requirements for people of faith! But Jesus had already declared all food clean (Mark 7:19), and subsequent events with the Gentiles reveal that Peter's experience had nothing to do with their diet. Clearly, something else was at play. As we've seen, most dream-visions are symbolic. Objects and imagery are used to communicate a message. In this case, the food on the tablecloth clearly represents the Gentiles – the people who Jews had long believed were 'unclean'.

The other symbol in the vision is the voice from heaven. The fact that Peter hears it coming from above points to the idea that it belongs to God. This is why the scene is so confusing for Peter. Why would the God of Israel be saying something different to Peter from what he had said to Moses? And yet this is what the Holy Spirit seemed to be saying: it's now acceptable to welcome the Gentiles into the people of God! Or, in Peter's words to his visitors, 'You are well aware that it is against our law for a Jew to associate with or visit a Gentile. But God has shown me that I should not call anyone impure or unclean' (Acts 10:28).

The meaning of the vision is now clear. From our vantage point, it seems obvious, but for Peter, it took time to understand. God was saying that the good news of Jesus was not just for his people, but for *every* nation – even the despised Romans. Peter's call to build the church was to include the Jews as well as those formerly outside the covenant – the Gentiles. It was a message that would go on to change the world.

Where Did Peter's Dream Come From?

The fourth question of our framework highlights the source of the dream: *Where did Peter's dream come from?* Himself, other spirits or God?

To begin with, we can see it's highly improbable that Peter's experience arose from himself since it would have contradicted everything he knew and believed. The other two options are that it came from other spirits – perhaps the Enemy seeking to destroy God's covenant with the Jews – or that it came from God.

Ultimately, Peter concluded that his vision of the unappetizing lunch came from God. His story provides us with a pattern to follow when we seek to identify the source of our own dream-visions. There are three criteria that become evident as we look more closely at Peter's story. They allow us to test the message of the dream to see if it is from God (1 John 4:1). These criteria can be framed in the form of questions.[1]

The first and most important test question in discerning a God-dream or vision asks: 'Would Jesus say this?' Peter knew that when Holy Spirit spoke, it would be as Jesus' continuing voice. That is, everything the Spirit said would be consistent with the words and actions of Jesus. God's message would reflect Jesus' character as the perfect revelation of the invisible God (Col. 1:15) and continue Jesus' ministry and mission on the earth (John 16:7,13).

For Peter then, the question became: would Jesus have said the good news was for the Gentiles, too? Would Jesus have said that they could be 'clean' in God's eyes?

We know that Jesus spent most of his earthly ministry with Jews, but that he also came into contact with Gentiles. When he did, he reached out to them with acceptance and love. For example, he healed a Roman centurion's son (Luke 7:1–10), cast out an evil spirit from a Gadarene man (Luke 8:26–39) and freed the demon-possessed daughter of a Canaanite woman (Matt. 15:21–28). Then, before he left the earth, he gathered his disciples together and commissioned them to go into *the world* and make disciples of *all* nations (Matt. 28:19). When later reflecting on his vision, Peter *remembered* the things Jesus had said (Acts 11:16). So, in response to the question 'Would Jesus say this?', Peter could have only answered 'Yes'.

Assessing our dream-visions against the character and nature of Jesus is the most important criterion for determining its source. But there are two other criteria also evident in Peter's experience. You see them further along in the story.

To begin with, Peter's experience involved the witness of another person. So while Peter was hearing God's voice on the rooftop, God was speaking to Cornelius as well. The timing is impeccable. It was as if God brought them together so they could compare notes: *Peter, what did you see? Cornelius, what did you hear?* When they saw that God was speaking the same message to both of them, they knew it was from God.

This is the beauty of God-conversations under the New Covenant. All those who choose to follow Jesus receive his Spirit and can hear directly from God for themselves. This means God can confirm his messages through another person. When he does so, we find an objective way of assessing our interpretations. The source of our dream-visions becomes clearer when God speaks twice. Thus, our second test question becomes: 'Is someone else saying this?'

The final question for discernment for Peter is borne out in the events that followed Peter's visit to Cornelius's home. There Peter began sharing the good news of Jesus with the Gentiles. As he did, the Holy Spirit fell on them in the same way as he did for Jews (Acts 10:44–47)! This was a tangible *sign* that God endorsed Peter's message. The power and blessing of God followed the message of his vision.

This, then, was the answer to the third test question: 'Are spiritual signs following this?' God's messages in dream-visions

Peter's Vision of an Unappetizing Lunch

will always be followed by signs of divine presence and love. His words are a reflection of his character and nature. They bear his authority and have the power to bring themselves to pass (Gen. 1:3; Isa. 55:11; John 6:63). As such, they will always further the kingdom of God whenever received and acted upon. Spiritual signs include previously unknown information that is later verified, miracles, healing, freedom, and the fruit of God's Spirit such as love, joy and peace (Gal. 5:22–23). In other words, true messages from God will have the *same impact* as Jesus' ministry.

Peter's God-conversation gives us the pattern for testing our own dream-visions. In seeking to identify their source, we should ask the following three questions of discernment:

1. Would Jesus say this?
2. Is someone else saying this?
3. Are spiritual signs following this?

If the answer to each of our questions is 'Yes', we know the dream-vision is from God.

05 What Was the Dream Asking Peter to Do?

The final question in the God Dreams framework looks at what the dream is calling for in response, or in Peter's case, what the dream was asking Peter to do.

Having understood that the church should include Gentiles as well as Jews, Peter was now called to outwork this in his ministry. It was a clear directive, but it wasn't easy to do. For Peter, it meant defying the traditions and customs he had been raised with. It meant moving into unfamiliar social circles and engaging in practices that were new and uncomfortable.

Then there was opposition. People do not change easily and not everyone understood the message of Peter's dream-vision. Later, the resistance became so strong that Peter withdrew from the Gentiles, and Paul had to rebuke him! (Gal. 2:11–12). Ultimately, though, Peter's obedience to the message of his vision led to the rise of the global church, millions of transformed lives and the ongoing fulfilment of Jesus' mission to reach the entire world. Indeed, Peter's story demonstrates the impact that all God-dreams will have when we respond to them in faith and submission. When we act in accordance with the Holy Spirit, we will see the manifestation of God's plans. As Jesus promised, blessing will flow to those who 'hear the word of God and obey it' (Luke 11:28).

Your Customized Dream Dictionary

The Yellow Peacock

Becky was praying for a teenager at a church meeting when the image of a yellow peacock formed in her mind. Becky had no idea what it meant. What was significant about a yellow peacock? Perhaps the vision was about *beauty* since peacocks are known for their appearance . . . A *flair for performance* since they like to proudly display their feathers? Or maybe a *promise of happiness* because of the colour yellow . . .?

Lost for clarity, Becky asked the woman she was praying for, 'Does a yellow peacock mean anything to you?'

The woman's face lit up immediately. 'That's my password!' She went on to explain how 'yellow peacock' was the password for *everything* in her life – her computer, social media and personal accounts.

As they reflected on the vision together, the message of the yellow peacock became clear. God was revealing his deep and intimate knowledge of the young woman's life. He *knew* her in a way no one else could! The Holy Spirit was also asking for open access to her heart. Would she grant it? The image of a yellow peacock was a powerful reminder of God's omniscience as well as his desire for intimate relationship.

In Chapter 6, we introduced the nature of symbolism in the third question of our God Dreams framework. In order to understand our dream-visions, we need to learn the language of pictures and imagery. We need to think *symbolically*. As in the story of the yellow peacock, the meaning is not always clear at first. As with learning any language, proficiency takes time and practice.

In the yellow peacock vision, we also see how symbols are tailored to their audience. The meaning of the yellow peacock was specific to this woman's life. In this chapter, we explore the dynamic of symbolism in more detail. We discover the contextual nature of symbols, how they can bear multiple meanings and how to know which is right.

Thinking Symbolically

We begin with an exercise to help us think symbolically.

For each of the following five pictures, write down what you think of when you see it. Don't write what you actually see; think of what you associate with the image and how it makes you *feel*.

Your Customized Dream Dictionary

Picture 1

Picture 2

Picture 3

Picture 4

Picture 5

How did you do? Perhaps when you saw Picture 1, you thought of *freedom*, because eagles fly so majestically in the sky. Or maybe you thought of *vision* because eagles are known for their exceptionally good eyesight. Or perhaps you felt *peace* because eagles have a special ability to rise above storms.

What about Picture 2: the waterfall? Did you sense *cleansing* from the rushing waters? Or maybe a loud *noise* as the water plummeted down the cliff?

This is what it means to think symbolically!

Now ask another person to do the same exercise and compare your answers. What do you notice?

It is likely that your responses to each picture will not be the same. Consider Picture 3. The lion may represent danger to one person, but royalty to another. Similarly, Picture 4: the rock climber may invoke fear in one but a sense of adventure in another. Or what about Picture 5? Is it a sunset or a sunrise? A beginning or an ending? Which is correct?

The answer of course is *neither*, or *all*, or *none*! For the most part, symbols in dream-visions are tailored to their audience. That means interpretation will vary according to the person viewing it. The question is 'What do the symbols mean to *you* – the dreamer?' This is the beauty of symbolism as well as its complexity!

Consider another symbol that functions in multiple ways. A cat. Now if *I* dream about a cat, I think of comfort and joy. This is because I love cats. I own a gorgeous grey Burmese called Gucci who feeds off cuddles and company. Whenever I think of cats, this is what I think of. But not everyone feels this way. If my brother saw a cat in his dream, warmth and joy would be the last thing he would associate with it. He would be more inclined to remove it from his house! Where I think *comfort*, he thinks *pest*. The symbol of a cat works differently for each of us.

There are also other interpretations for a cat that vary according to the receiving culture. For example, if you were an ancient Egyptian, seeing a cat in a vision would be a welcome omen, since in Egypt, cats were considered sacred and bore a special connection to the gods. But if you lived in medieval times, a cat would provoke the opposite association. Instead of reverence or hope, you would feel suspicion and fear (particularly if the cat was black).

This example also shows how symbols can carry a shared meaning for a group of people. A good example is the image of a red cross. This symbol came into existence more than 150 years ago when it was adopted by the Geneva Conventions and the Red Cross organization. It is flown on the battlefield in times of war and literally means 'Don't shoot!' The red cross signifies protection, humanitarian aid and impartial assistance for anyone who needs it.[1] In other words, it represents safety and help.

That is, if you are from the western part of the world. If, however, you found yourself wounded on a battlefield in the Middle East, you wouldn't be looking for a red cross – you'd be looking for a red *crescent*. This is because the countries of the Middle East are predominantly Muslim. Hence, the symbol of a crescent rather than a cross is used to communicate safety and refuge in line with Islamic tradition.

At an even wider level, a symbol can carry one meaning for humanity as a whole. I call such images the 'ABCs of symbols'. The ABCs are universal across all cultures and tend to be the most common symbols in our dreams. They include houses and rooms, vehicles, animals, birthing and babies, death and dying, clothing and nakedness, teeth, colours, numbers and people. We will explore them in more detail in the next chapter.

Your Dream Vocabulary

Over time and as particular symbols recur, you will find yourself establishing your own 'dream vocabulary'. That is, you'll be able to recognize how particular symbols function for you.

Several years after my 'thief in the night' dream (Chapter 1), I had a second dream involving a thief. You may recall that in the first dream a thief had broken into my home and stolen some of my valuables while I slept. God was saying: *Stay 'awake', be ready and prepare in faith for my plans to be fulfilled – even when you don't know the timing.* In the second dream of the thief, the scene was similar apart from one detail. This time, the thief entered my home, but I woke up! I called the police, but the thief got away.

The message of this dream was easy to interpret. Like the first dream, it still wasn't the right time for God's promises to be fulfilled, but on this occasion, I'd woken up! The dream brought a message of encouragement. It was saying that God's time was still coming and I was closer to being ready.

Ironically enough, a third dream followed several years later. Unlike the first two dreams, on this occasion I knew the time *before* the thief arrived and was able to catch him before he stole anything. Now it was time, and I was ready! In each vision, the same symbols were used.

This pattern is true for all of us. Once you've learned to interpret your dream-visions, you will begin to develop your own dream vocabulary. Over time, certain symbols are likely to appear again and again. You will be able to compile a 'dictionary' of symbols specific to you.

This is why it's important not to rely too heavily on published dream dictionaries. You may have seen them in bookstores. They provide a sort of anthology of symbols. As in a dictionary, you look up the symbol to find a list of meanings. But the problem is knowing which is the right one. The meanings can be as diverse as our imagination and the cultures from which we come. As in the example of the cat, is it a comfort or is it a pest? Is it a good omen or bad?

Dream dictionaries can help us think symbolically, but they are limited in their use, since the meaning of symbols depends on their intended audience. It is wiser to learn the *skill* of thinking symbolically in the context of your own life, rather than merely referencing a book without context. The question must always be: what does the symbol mean to *you*?

The Symbols of Biblical Dream-Visions

An understanding of the contextual nature of symbols also applies to the dream-visions of the Bible. In the same way that dream-visions employ symbols that make sense to us, God employed symbols that made sense to the original audience – that is, the Jewish people in the Ancient Near Eastern world of the Old Testament and the Christian church in the Greco-Roman world of the New Testament. God is a masterful communicator who tailors the message to his audience.

This is the reason why many of the God-conversations in Scripture are filled with symbols that are distinctly Jewish. Some of these may be familiar to us; others not. For example, think of Zechariah's dream about the two olive trees and the seven-branched lampstand. As the grandson of a high priest, these images carried a powerful meaning for Zechariah who would have encountered them regularly. The same is true for John's dream-visions at the time of the early church in the book of Revelation. As we'll see later (Chapters 10–11), John's visions of strange hybrid creatures and a seven-headed dragon were not uncommon in the ancient world. In fact, the image of a dragon was well known throughout the Ancient Near East and usually represented the forces of evil and chaos. This is why knowing the biblical setting is crucial. Ignoring it leads us down a dubious path. Some have interpreted the winged locusts in John's visions (Rev. 9) as helicopters![2] Not only is this interpretation wildly illogical since helicopters didn't exist in the first century; it also completely distorts the message of the vision.

Understanding the contextual nature of symbols also means that we shouldn't use our Bibles as a sort of dream dictionary. Just because Zechariah's vision of an olive tree signified an anointed leader in Scripture *does not mean* that every tree in every dream-vision symbolizes an anointed leader. The olive tree had a particular meaning for the Jewish people in Zechariah's day that may or may not transfer to a non-Jewish culture. The dreams of the biblical characters are best applied when we understand them in the context of *their* time.

Of course, once we're familiar with the biblical symbols, God may well use them to speak to us. For example, God may use the symbols of 'oil, milk and honey' to bring a message of prosperity in our own life in the same way he used it for the Israelites on their journey to the promised land.

We can also study Scripture to see how God used symbolic language to speak to his people. This was the approach we applied in our study of Peter's vision of the unappetizing lunch. It is also the approach we'll use later when we learn from John's dream-visions in Revelation. The insights gained not only reveal Holy Spirit's message to the church but also assist us in our own God-conversations.

Our ever-present assumption is that God wants to communicate with us clearly and effectively. God is not hiding, but desires to reveal himself to us in ways we understand, using the metaphors, idioms and imagery familiar to us. It's then that we can follow.

Handle with Care

If a symbol can carry several meanings, how do we know which is the right one?

A woman once told me her dream. She saw herself getting married a second time. In the dream, there were two wedding dresses on offer. One was clean and white; the other was covered in dirty brown stains. Then she heard a voice telling her to put the clean dress on because it was meant for her.

At the time, the woman was experiencing difficulties in her marriage; she and her husband were seeing a counsellor to help work through their problems. How was she to understand the dream? There are two possible interpretations – each with the opposite message! One pointed to the restoration of the woman's marriage. Where it was 'stained', God could make it new. An alternative interpretation pointed to a second marriage, another man and a new relationship. One related to restoration; the other to divorce and remarriage. Which one was it?

This example demonstrates the complex nature of symbolism as well as the implications of getting it wrong. The woman could have easily overlaid the dream's message with her own ideas and desires. This is why it is crucial to handle our visionary experiences with care.

It is also why we should seek the help of Holy Spirit. As Joseph said to the Egyptian pharaoh when contemplating his dream of the skinny and fat cows, God is the ultimate source of wisdom (Gen. 41:15–16), and interpretations *belong* to him (Gen. 40:8). Daniel too emulated this posture when he sought the God who alone 'reveals mysteries' in the interpretation of a dream that had troubled the Babylonian king (Dan. 2:26–28).

Dream-vision interpretation requires patience and caution. We should not rush to get the meaning right, particularly when it isn't explicit. Understanding is a *process*. It involves prayer, reflection and orientation towards God. Consultation with those who know us well is also crucial. And we must never forget to test the source of our dream-visions.

Fortunately, the woman in this story took time to pray about her dream of the two wedding dresses. She concluded that the first interpretation was the correct one. So she persevered in her marriage and exercised faith in the God who had promised to restore it. As time passed, she experienced the outworking of her vision; it was like getting married anew as the dirty stains of her relationship were washed away.

A literal dream?

Caution is also called for when considering if our dreams may not be symbolic at all. While in the vast majority of cases, dream-visions speak symbolically, at times they can be literal.

This was true of my mother's dream of my grandfather. Grandpa really did die while sleeping in his favourite chair. So how do we know the difference?

It is wise to always begin with the assumption that our dream-vision is symbolic. Most dreams are about *us*. If you were to see someone dying in your dream, it doesn't mean you should immediately inform them of their impending death! It is more likely to be some*thing* dying in *your* life rather than a pronouncement about someone else.

However, in a small number of cases, a dream may be literal. We may be alerted to an issue in the life of another, catch a literal glimpse of the future or be warned about an impending incident. In one case, a friend saw a vision of a father sexually assaulting his child when staying overnight in his home. After careful investigation, the vision was proved to be true and the child was able to receive protection from further abuse.

Distinguishing between a symbolic and literal dream takes care and discernment. Wisdom calls us again to reflect, pray and consult the Holy Spirit. We need to share our experiences with those who know us, and ensure our interpretations are in line with Jesus. We may also need to wait until time reveals more. Whether symbolically or literally, God speaks to be understood. If the message is from God, he will make it clear.

The 'Aha' Moment!

If you were to ask several people to interpret a dream-vision, they would probably come up with a whole range of different answers. This means that even though the best way to interpret our experiences is to do so in consultation with others, we as the dreamer are *always* the final interpreter. When we receive the right meaning, it will sit well with us. This is the 'aha' moment. It's a sense of 'That's it!' We *know* it's right.

During one of my God Dreams seminars, an elderly woman suddenly shouted out in the middle of the class, 'I know what it means!' With tears flowing down her cheeks, she went on to explain. Ever since her husband had died ten years earlier, she'd been having a recurring dream. In the dream, she was waiting for him to pick her up in their car. When he arrived, she got into the back seat and waited for him to drive off. But her husband remained in the back seat, so the car went nowhere. She kept waiting for him to take the wheel, but he didn't. Then she woke up.

Now she understood. The dream was telling her to *get into the driver's seat* – her husband was not coming back for her. She wiped away her tears and with light in her eyes said, 'Now I know what I need to do.'

This woman had experienced her 'aha' moment. The message resonated deeply and gave her the impetus to change her life.

When faced with a variety of options, this is the moment we're looking for. With the right interpretation comes a sense of 'Aha, that's it!' The dream will make sense. It will resonate with us and fill us with understanding. When we respond to it, it may even have the capacity to change our lives.

The ABCs of Symbols

Snakes on the Rooftop

Dream-visions can highlight the most subtle messages in exaggerated and theatrical ways. This was the case in one of my dreams. At the time, I'd been doing well in life – I was settled in my home and enjoying my job. I felt as though I was dealing with the everyday challenges with confidence and strength. But then one day, a good friend said some things that rocked my faith. Though well-meaning, their words brought doubt and a sense of trepidation about God's plans for my life. For a moment, I'd listened to them, feeling the weight of their discouragement. They niggled at me and I began toying with the idea of lowering my expectations.

Then I had a dream. I saw myself standing outside my childhood home. It felt familiar and safe. Suddenly, to my horror, I noticed an enormous snake stretched out along the rooftop of the house. It looked like one of those giant boa constrictors that swallow you in one mouthful. In the dream, I panicked: *Someone get rid of the snake!*

But almost immediately, with great relief, I realized it was okay because the snake was *on the rooftop*. There was no need to worry since it was outside the house.

Then I saw something move. Alarm bells rang in my head as a baby snake appeared from underneath the body of its mother. It slithered along the top of the roof, down the side of the doorway and under the crack of the door.

I screamed, *Quick! Get the snake out of my house!*

The next thing I saw was a giant hammer. It swung down from high above and crushed the head of the baby snake.

Then I woke up.

My dream of the snakes on the rooftop powerfully communicated a warning about my thought-life via two of the most common symbols found in dreams. You'll notice the house, and then the imagery of an animal. Houses and animals belong to a small group of symbols I call the 'ABCs'. Even though symbols can carry a range of meanings depending on their context, the ABCs bear a generic meaning across all cultures and people groups. They are the symbols that appear in most of our dreams, and they largely mean the same thing. In this chapter, we will explore them one by one. Knowing our ABCs will give us the basics for interpreting the vast majority of our dreams.

Houses and Rooms

Houses and rooms are a frequent feature of our dreams. Houses normally represent our life, and its rooms signify different

The ABCs of Symbols

aspects of it. The symbol makes sense, given that our home is our main habitat and the vantage point for everything we experience in our lives. Hence, the appearance of houses and rooms in dream-visions will often point to what is happening in and around us – the good and the bad, and that which is seen and unseen.

So, when you see a house in a dream, ask: Whose house is it? What state is it in? How many floors are there? Is the house being moved into or out of? Who is living in the house? Who should be living there and who shouldn't be? What rooms do you see?

Perhaps it's a different house you're moving into, and a new season is imminent. Maybe your home is rundown and you need some self-care. Perhaps there are people in your living room who should be moved into the front yard as you establish healthier boundaries. Or maybe there's an intruder in your life who needs to be shown the door.

Your childhood home may also appear. This often represents a time of innocence, the hopes you had as a child, or perhaps difficult times growing up. In my dream about the snake on the rooftop, the house was from my childhood and represented my hopes for the future.

The rooms of a home in a dream usually point to specific areas of our lives. A bedroom likely indicates a place of intimacy, reflecting the state of our closest relationships. A bathroom is the place where we clean up, so may point to a need for cleansing or healing. A darkened basement probably represents the hidden parts of our life, tucked away from the public eye.

Jesus used the symbol of a house when he spoke of how to build a strong and stable life. A person who builds their life on God's words is like a house built on a rock. This life can withstand storms. But a person who chooses to reject God's words is like a house on sand. It will fall apart in a storm (Matt. 7:24,26).

Part of the reason why houses and rooms are so common in our dream-visions is because they speak to us about our lives. The message is likely to be personal, perhaps hidden from others and deeply significant.

Vehicles

Vehicles appear frequently in our dreams. They include cars, trains, aeroplanes, buses, bicycles and the like. A good example can be seen in my dream about the corpses along the highway, when the car I was driving hit a traffic jam.

To understand the meaning of vehicles, think about what they *do*. Vehicles transport us from one place to another. They are the means by which we reach a given destination. Therefore, in most cases, vehicles symbolize our job, career or some other significant pursuit.

Once we've understood the general meaning of vehicles, it's helpful to consider the specifics. Ask: What kind of vehicle is it? Is it a bus, with others riding with you, or are you going solo as you do on a bike? How fast or slow is the vehicle travelling? What condition is it in? Are *you* driving, or is someone else at the wheel? Should you be in that vehicle or is it time to change to another? Have you arrived at your destination or are you only halfway there?

A woman once told me about a recurring dream featuring her car: 'I am driving so fast that I crash.' When I asked her why she crashed, she said it was because the car hadn't been well maintained. My next question was: 'How fast-paced is your life right now?' The woman blushed with acknowledgement, knowing what she needed to do.

In my own life, vehicles have often been used to convey a message about my ministry career. In one dream, I saw myself travelling on a train. I fell asleep, and when I woke up, I was on a bus. I had *changed vehicles*. Then I literally woke up.

The meaning of the dream was clear and I drove to work that day mentally preparing for it: *My job is about to change, my job is about to change*. Sure enough, later that week, my boss called me into his office. Unbeknown to me, he had been working on a restructure of the organisation. 'I need to change your job,' he said. 'It's like we've been on a train, but now we've changed vehicles!'

Animals

Animals are another common feature of dream-visions. They make for useful symbols because of their many diverse qualities. In deciphering the meaning of an animal, ask what features it is known for. A bulldog may symbolize tenacity; a parrot, mimicry; a butterfly, dramatic change; or a fox, slyness.

In a vision, a woman saw a deer bending down to drink from a pool of water. But the deer's antlers kept getting in its way and stopped it from drinking. We know that the antlers of a deer are used for defence. As we reflected on the vision together, the woman realized that certain defence mechanisms had developed in her heart and prevented her from receiving the healing God had for her.

The meaning of my dream about the snakes on the rooftop also becomes clear when you recognize the features snakes are known for. Here, the snakes represented deception and lies. While I'd been successful in rejecting the 'big snake' in dealing with the bigger issues of my life, the vision showed how a 'little snake' had penetrated my thinking when I had briefly entertained the lies of my well-meaning but sceptical friend. The little snake also warned of the consequences. Even the smallest of unhelpful thoughts need to be destroyed before they grow larger! Interestingly, Scripture draws on similar imagery. Satan – the 'father of lies' (John 8:44) – is often depicted as a snake (Gen. 3:1–5,15; Rev. 12:9), whose 'head' Jesus would later 'crush'. (Note, too, that snakes can also signify a vastly different meaning. They represent 'healing' in Israel's story [Num. 21:8–9] and in the logo for the Hippocratic Oath taken by doctors at the beginning of their careers.)

Babies and Birthing

Have you ever given birth in a dream? Even men can be pregnant in dreams! What does the symbol of babies and birthing mean?

Whenever a child is born, there is new life, along with a sense of excitement and fresh opportunities. Babies are a clever way of signifying new beginnings.

The ABCs of Symbols

If you've dreamt of a baby, first consider what the baby represents. Is anything new beginning in your life? A new project? New job? New relationship?

Then consider the state of the baby. Perhaps the baby has just been conceived and a new endeavour has recently been conceptualized. Or maybe the baby is fully grown and ready to be birthed. The baby might be premature if the timing isn't right for birthing yet. If the baby is still in the womb, how is the pregnancy going? Is the baby well-formed? Is anything stopping it from being born? Or has the baby miscarried or been aborted?

The baby may have already been born. Was the labour short or long? Who is looking after the baby now? What state of growth is it in? Is it someone else's baby or your own?

The symbol of a baby is used powerfully in Ancient Israel's story. The prophet Isaiah saw a vision of a barren woman who symbolized the state of Israel. As a people exiled in Babylon and far from her homeland, she had failed to birth God's promises in her life. But God was telling her to sing because one day her 'child' would be born (Isa. 54:1). In other words, one day Israel would return to her homeland.

In my own life, God used the symbol of a baby to represent the beginning of a new season in my ministry career. The dream showed that I had given birth. It was an easy labour and, to my joy, the newborn was perfectly formed. But then the baby smiled – and it had a full set of teeth! I was shocked. Even in my dream, I knew babies weren't born with teeth. *What was wrong with my baby?!*

Then it got worse. In the next scene, the baby had suddenly grown and stood a metre tall – a giant baby on its own two feet.

The next thing I knew, we were at an indoor swimming pool. Someone took my baby from me, walked to the far side of the pool and threw it into the water. I screamed, 'You can't do that to my baby! It will drown!'

I peered into the pool, fearing the worst. Suddenly my baby's head popped out of the water. It was swimming with confidence and smiling happily.

The meaning of the dream became apparent on my first ministry trip for God Conversations. I was sitting in the front row of a large church in Germany, about to speak in a foreign setting for the first time. It was a two-hour seminar with all new content and I would be speaking through a translator. When they announced my name, I panicked: *I can't do this!* I was way out of my depth. I stepped up to the platform terrified. But strangely, the moment I began speaking, it felt familiar and easy – as if I'd been doing it for years. My ministry was brand new, yet unusually mature. The baby was swimming and happy. My vision of seeing it being 'thrown into the deep end' captured the situation perfectly.

Death and Dying

In the same way that the symbol of babies and birthing represents *beginnings*, death and dying represents *endings*.

Death in a dream most commonly refers to the end of something significant – the termination of a job or position, the death of an old way of life, or the end of a relationship.

When death and dying appears in your dream-visions, ask: What is ending or finishing in my life? What needs to have closure? Is there hope for the dying or is it time to bury the dead?

The symbol of death features in my 'corpses on the highway' dream. Multiple corpses signified the demise of my hopes and promises. Death is an effective way to communicate the grief and hopelessness associated with loss.

The symbol of death is also prominent in Ezekiel's vision of dry bones (Ezek. 37:1–14). Here, the bones represented the death of Israel's hopes for the future. Fortunately, the vision showed a renewal of the promise when the skeletons were revived and took on flesh again.

As we've seen, death in dream-visions can also be literal. In my PhD studies, a woman shared a dream of her grandmother's passing on the other side of the world. She later discovered that her grandma had died at the exact moment of the vision. The dream brought deep comfort, particularly as she was unable to attend the funeral. My mother had a similar experience with her father in his chair. Dreams of death and dying are not uncommon. At the same time, it is best to remember that most are symbolic rather than literal.

Clothing and Nakedness

The symbols of clothing and nakedness are another common element of dream-visions. Can you guess what they mean?

In our waking lives, the clothing we wear reflects our identity or role. A police officer wears a uniform of authority. A priest wears a collar of consecration. A nurse wears an outfit of care and compassion. The outer garb points to the inner person.

In your dream, ask: What type of clothing was being worn? Were there any particular features that stood out? Did the clothes fit, or were they too big so that you had to grow into them? Perhaps they were too small, and you need to change. Maybe there's a whole new outfit to put on in preparation for a different role.

The symbol of clothing is beautifully illustrated in one of Zechariah's visions during the time of Israel's exile. God's plan was to lead the nation back to their homeland under the leadership of Joshua the high priest. But Joshua was ill-equipped for the task, so God 'changed his outfit', saying: 'Take off his filthy clothes . . . See, I have taken away your sin, and I will put fine garments on you' (Zech. 3:3–4). Joshua's new robes vividly represented his call to rebuild the temple of Jerusalem.

In my own life, clothing has been a recurring symbol. When God first called me into ministry, he used the symbol of the royal mantle worn by the biblical character Esther. Esther had been a young Jewish orphan exiled in Persia when she became queen. Her unexpected appointment was later instrumental in saving her people. In one of my visions, Esther's royal robes were hanging on a mannequin ready for me to wear, but I was reluctant to put them on. Like Esther, I had to embrace my divinely appointed role even though the outfit change was unexpected – at the time I was a sports teacher accustomed to wearing tracksuits! A subsequent vision revealed Esther's robes to be too big for me; it would take time to grow into God's calling on my life.

In the same way that clothing represents the roles we take on or the identity we associate with, nakedness can signify a loss of identity or a sense of inadequacy for a role. This is why we turn up naked in a dream when feeling ill-prepared for a task!

Nakedness carries other meanings too. It may indicate a sense of exposure as our vulnerability is on display. It may also point to a desire for intimacy – often expressed as sexual activity – as we shed the attire that covers our true selves.

Teeth

Have you ever had a dream where your teeth are falling out? It's a horrible feeling! Losing your teeth brings a profound sense of helplessness and loss. So, what do teeth represent?

Consider the role teeth play in your life. It's very difficult to eat without them. Teeth are our bodies' equipment, giving us the power to ingest food and ultimately survive. It should not be surprising, then, that our teeth usually represent our capacity to achieve. They are like the working tools of our lives – our skills, talents and abilities.

If teeth appear in your dreams, ask: What state are they in? Are they old and falling out or are they new and maturing? Are there any missing? Can you use them properly?

A friend of mine has experienced recurring teeth dreams throughout her life. In the scenes, her mouth is full of chewing gum, and she is trying to pull it out – often to no avail.

Over and over she sees herself struggling unsuccessfully with great gobs of gum, her mouth so full she is unable to speak. When she wakes up, she is tired and frustrated. Through the years, my friend has realized that the dream is often connected with a sense of disempowerment in her workplace, particularly in times of conflict where it's been difficult to use her voice. It may be of no surprise, then, that as she has skilled herself in new ways of communicating with wisdom and discretion, the amount of chewing gum in her teeth dreams has increasingly lessened! The dreams have also become less frequent.

A dream about teeth came at a critical time in my own life. In the scene, all my teeth were falling out. Panicked, I rushed to find a dentist. *Quick, I've got to get my teeth back in!* But when the dentist inspected my mouth, he discovered a whole new set of baby teeth growing underneath! There was no need to replace the old teeth since the new ones were almost in place.

The dream pointed to my struggle to transition out of an old season and into the new. At the time, I'd been holding on to the vestiges of a former job even while I knew that a new and better one was coming. It was time to let the old teeth fall out and trust that the new ones would be ready to go.

Teeth can also represent wisdom and maturity. Pathologists use teeth in autopsies to investigate the age of an unknown person. You may have noticed this angle in my dream about the oversized baby. The rapid development of my ministry career was symbolized by the baby with a full set of teeth.

Colours

Colours are an effective way to communicate in dream-visions. Purple often represents royalty; green is fresh and full of life; red is the colour of passion.

A good example of how colour can operate symbolically is seen in John's visions in the book of Revelation. Here we see the saints of God wearing white robes that have been washed in blood (Rev. 7:14). How can clothing that has been washed in blood come out white?! Only when colour is operating as a symbol – in this case, red representing the blood of Jesus, and white signifying purity and righteousness.

Numbers

Numbers can operate symbolically too. The use of numbers to convey meaning was particularly prevalent in the ancient world where mathematical precision was less of a priority than it is for us. For example, the Ancient Sumerians used numbers to represent the quality of a king's reign. The higher the quality, the greater the number. Similarly in biblical history, numbers were used symbolically. This is probably the dynamic that is operating in the descriptions of characters such as Methuselah, who is said to have lived for 939 years (Gen. 5:27).

Furthermore, some numbers can carry specific meanings. In the biblical record, 3, 5, 7, 12 and 40 all feature prominently. For example, the number 40 is used to depict a time of testing (as in Noah's flood and the wilderness sojourns of Israel and Jesus). The number 7 is used to symbolize perfection and completion (as in the days of creation) and contrasts with 6, the number of humanity. The number 1,000 is used in the book of Revelation to denote a very long, perhaps infinite, period of time.

People

What does it mean when *people* appear in our dreams? This symbol is one of the most important since it appears frequently, yet is often misunderstood. A variety of people may feature in our dreams – our parents or siblings, a friend from school, an ex-romantic partner, a celebrity, a work colleague or someone you knew from many years ago.

From the outset, it's helpful to know that when we see people in our dreams, the message is *not* usually about them. It is more likely to be about *us*. As with other images in our dreams, people function symbolically. Their presence is likely to refer to some part of ourselves. This is why psychologists often use the term 'shadow figures' to describe them. The person is acting as a symbol, reflecting the shadow part of ourselves we don't always see.

So we ask: What do you associate with the person? What role do they play in your life? What do you think of when you see them? What are they encouraging you to do?

For example, the appearance of your mother may relate to your maternal instinct. A pastor may represent the will of God. A hero or someone you hold in high esteem may reflect your aspirations or a desire to display the same qualities. Someone you feared in your past may point to the fear you carry in yourself, or someone with an anger problem may point to your own struggles in that area. For many years, a childhood friend repeatedly appeared in my dreams. Each time, she represented my childhood hopes and dreams.

People may also appear in our dreams in a sexual way. While there may be physical causes, this is not always the case. The sexual act is an expression of intimacy and union. Sexual activity may therefore represent your inner longings, and the person would thus symbolize what you might be longing for.

There may also be times when the appearance of another person in our dreams carries a prophetic message for them. God may be calling us to pass on a message for their strengthening, encouragement and comfort (1 Cor. 14:3). We will look at this phenomenon in Chapter 15.

***

Symbols such as houses, vehicles, animals, babies and people are the building blocks of dream language and give us the formative elements for interpretation. Knowing the ABCs of symbols helps us to understand most of our dreams.

Once we understand the basics, we can move on to more complex dream-visions. In this, the Bible gives us some breathtaking examples. Just as we've explored Peter's dream-vision on the rooftop in Joppa, we now turn to the most vivid and colourful visions in biblical history – those described by John in the book of Revelation.

John's Vision of the Heavenly Government

Imagine. It's Sabbath day in the late first century CE. You're gathered with your church community in a large home in the city of Pergamum. Psalms have been sung, a meal has been shared, and now one of your group is speaking. They're reading a letter from John, who has been exiled by the Romans on the island of Patmos. John has a message from God that he feels is important for your church and others in the region. You attend carefully to the Spirit's words, exhorting you to stay faithful to Jesus. The message is both encouraging and sobering. In some ways, your community has done well. In others, there is room for improvement.

The letter goes on to describe a vivid scene. It's the throne room of heaven! There's a crystal floor, a gathering of unusual creatures and leaders, and a throne encircled by a rainbow. You listen in awe as John details the otherworldly scene. It was the first of many that would arrest your attention. John's words powerfully communicate God's heart for your situation and are particularly

John's Vision of the Heavenly Government 137

significant given the high price he is paying for his faith. You continue to ponder his message in the days to come . . .

* * *

Since John's visions were first shared among the churches of Asia Minor, they have been preserved for us as the last book of the Bible, Revelation. God had spoken to John through a series of visions and called him to pass them on to the church in Pergamum and at least six other churches in the area. The visions took the church members behind the scenes of their day-to-day lives and showed them how to live as followers of Jesus under the shadow of the Roman Empire. It was a challenging and confronting message that would go on to help shape the nature of the early church.

However, when we read John's visions today, the message isn't quite as clear as it was for the Christians of Asia Minor. For us, the book of Revelation reads more like a chaotic mix of scenes from the *Lord of the Rings* than a portion of sacred Scripture! From a drunken prostitute straddling a seven-headed beast, to a river of blood that runs as deep as a horse's bridle, to a white-haired Jesus riding a horse with a sword in his mouth, it's not surprising that many today steer clear of the book and why some church leaders in history have even questioned its source.[1]

John's visions in Revelation provide us with a rich and elaborate demonstration of symbolic language. The images are many and complex. Some of them are interpreted for us. Others are more obscure and take time to work out. Some may not be decipherable at all, given that we are reading about them two thousand years later and don't have all the backstory.

Unfortunately, there has been a myriad of distorted and misleading interpretations of John's visions throughout history. As we've seen, dream-visions can have multiple meanings, and today they're not difficult to find. Pick up a commentary on Revelation and you will discover any number of angles. Many of these have emerged because interpreters haven't fully understood the language of symbolism and how dream-visions work.[2] Some of the more popular material makes a radical departure from the teachings of the historic church.[3] Tragically, these interpretations have often been damaging to Christian witness, provoking conspiracy theories, unfounded fears and, ultimately, un-Christlike behaviour.[4]

In this chapter, we apply our interpretative skills to the opening scene of John's dream-visions – the heavenly throne room (Rev. 4 – 5). We use the first three questions of the God Dreams framework to explore the setting, feelings and symbols of the scene. In subsequent chapters (13 and 14), we will address the fourth and fifth questions: source and response. Below, we apply the dream framework to several additional visions in John's experience (Chapters 11 and 12). Each discussion will teach us more about the interpretative process and help us better understand our own experiences.

It's important to remind ourselves at this point that due to the nature of symbolism, as well as our distance from the minds of the first-century audience, interpretations of Revelation are complex and myriad. However, while scholars debate the details, the basic message of Revelation in the light of Jesus' life and teachings is clear.

So, what did John see in this first and central scene of Revelation?

John's Vision of the Heavenly Government   139

The Lamb with Lion Power

The vision opens with the great throne-room in heaven. Featuring prominently is the throne, encircled by a brilliantly shining rainbow and surrounded by a crystal-clear sea of glass. Flashes of lightning and peals of thunder sound from the throne, and seven lamps blaze intensely in front of it.

Encircling the throne are twenty-four smaller thrones. On each sits an elder robed in white and wearing a gold crown. In the centre are four-winged creatures. One resembles a lion, another an eagle, the third an ox and the fourth a man. Their bodies are covered in eyes.

As John takes in the breathtaking scene, his attention is turned towards the One who sits on the throne. He has the appearance of jasper and ruby. In his right hand is a scroll, tightly secured with seven seals.

John hears a voice asking, 'Who can open the scroll?'

There is no answer.

The question is repeated: 'Who is worthy to break the seals?'

Still no answer.

John begins to weep uncontrollably. *Who can open the scroll? Someone must be found! Who is worthy to open it?*

Silence fills the room.

Suddenly, one of the elders cries out: 'Someone has been found!'

John is overcome with relief. But *who* is it?

'It's the Lion of the Tribe of Judah!'

John knows this lion. Of course! The one who was promised so long ago. The Messiah!

But then ... *What?*

It cannot be.

It's a *lamb*!

John watches as a small and fragile lamb takes centre stage. All eyes turn to see it walk meekly to the throne.

But look! The lamb is covered in blood! *Has it been slaughtered?*

And then ... *What?* John looks closer. The lamb has seven eyes! And seven horns?!

The scene erupts. The twenty-four elders remove the crowns from their heads and lower them to the ground. The winged creatures strum their harps and the whole gathering joins in with a mighty crescendo: 'Worthy, worthy is the lamb that was slain to receive power and wealth and wisdom and strength and honour and glory and praise!'

* * *

John's Vision of the Heavenly Government 141

It's a magnificent scene. Like the prophets of old, John had been invited by God into the divine council to 'see' and 'hear his word' (Jer. 23:18). Holy Spirit had 'pulled back the curtain' to reveal God's message about the government of heaven. But what was God saying?

As always, we start with the question of setting.

01 What Was Happening in the Life of John and the Asian Churches?

The message of John's vision only makes sense in the light of the time and place in which it came. If the visions of Revelation are God's 'answer' to his people, knowing the context will help us understand something of the question.

At a big-picture level, we must first remember *why* God speaks. Jesus said that Holy Spirit would remind God's people of himself (John 14:26) and then speak about things that were 'yet to come' (John 16:13); that is, he would apply the message of Jesus to their particular situation. This understanding provides us with the broader context of John's prophetic message. So, what about the specifics?

We know that the visions of Revelation were received by a leader named John, but there were several Johns in the early church and, unfortunately, we don't know *which* one it was.[5] Whether it was the apostle John or another leader of the same name, we can surmise that he was known to the churches of Roman-ruled Asia Minor (modern-day Turkey). After receiving his visions, he wrote them down and sent them to at least seven of these Christian communities.[6] Their specific locations are stated for us in the opening chapter of John's letter: Ephesus, Smyrna, Pergamum, Thyatira, Sardis, Philadelphia and Laodicea (Rev. 1:1–3). The churches lay on the major trade routes between Judea and Rome and were (probably) established by Paul and his missionary teams.[7] In addition (although we can't be sure), it's likely that at the time of John's visions, the emperor Domitian sat on the Roman throne.

The world of first-century Rome

So, what was it like for a Christian to live in Asia Minor under Domitian's rule?

As a first-century Christian, you lived in a world where Rome ruled supreme. Being a resident of one of its territories, you probably hadn't visited the capital, but you would still feel its presence wherever you went. Roman statues lined the streets, temples to the Roman gods sat high on the city mounts, and Roman festivals filled your calendar.

The empire's dominion also spread far beyond your region, extending into lands you only knew by name . . . over to Britannia in the west, the Germanic tribes to the north, down south to the desert fringes of northern Africa and then across the Mediterranean to Mesopotamia in the east. With so many lands and territories came great prosperity. Roman cities bustled with trade and activity, supported by a wide network of roads and shipping routes. *Pax Romana* – the 'peace of Rome' – was the order of the day, with Rome's authoritarian rule creating a great amassment of wealth and power. But all this prosperity came at

John's Vision of the Heavenly Government 143

a cost. Roman rule was exercised through violence, slavery and exploitation of the weak.[8] This was how ancient empires were built. Everything was done for the glory of Rome.

And who could all this success be attributed to? The one and only emperor, of course – the one who reigned at the hand of the gods. It was Emperor Augustus who had first introduced the idea of a divine leader at the turn of the century, but Domitian had taken it to the next level, introducing himself as *Dominus et Deus* – 'Lord and God'. Domitian demanded that his subjects see him as divine,[9] calling himself the 'world's sure salvation', 'blest protector and saviour',[10] even the 'King of Kings' and 'Lord of Lords'.[11] In every city of the empire, temples stood in his honour, sporting events paid homage to his name, and rituals, vows and sacrifices were practised to reinforce civic loyalty. The emperor's wealth, power and status were unsurpassed.

The life of a Christ-follower

It was in the midst of this world that you had made a decision to follow Jesus. Your church community was still in its infancy – part-Jewish and part-Gentile – with the events of Jesus' life only a generation or two in the past. In many ways, you were still working out what your new faith looked like in this polytheistic, multicultural world.

And then, not everyone understood the faith of your growing community. Even though Roman policy advocated for tolerance of the many religions under its rule, there was still plenty of misunderstanding. All peoples were required to worship the gods of Greece and Rome, except the Jews. Potential for persecution rumbled beneath the surface. John had already paid the price in exile, and there was talk that the situation might get worse.

You were also familiar with the stories from Emperor Nero's day, when Christians were blamed for the Great Fire of Rome that destroyed a third of the city. It was under Nero's rule that Christians were used as human torches in the royal palace and the beloved apostles Peter and Paul were executed. And of course, the memory of Jerusalem's fall in 70 CE was ever present, with stories of crucifixions, torture and bloodshed still fresh in the minds of many.[12] Like the destruction brought by Babylon of old, the decimation of the holy city and its temple by Roman soldiers had deeply scarred the collective memory. Everyone knew you didn't mess with Rome.

Amidst all this, how was a Christ-follower to live? Everywhere, Roman religious practices mingled with daily life, provoking difficult choices. In the marketplace, you might not be able to buy and sell without paying homage to the Roman gods. At parades and sports events, you could be accused of being unpatriotic if you refused to honour the emperor. What if you didn't comply? At best, you risked the rejection of family, friends and community. At worst, you could stoke the ire of local officials. Resistance seemed futile. How could a scattered minority compete with the might and grandeur of Rome? What difference could a small group of Christians make? A man named Antipas had already stood up for his faith and paid the ultimate price (Rev. 2:13).

Added to all this was the threat of persecution from the Jews. Even though Jesus had been a Jew and much of your heritage sprang from his tradition, local Jews now viewed you with suspicion and contempt. They were angered not only by your beliefs about Jesus, but also by the Christian push to join them in claiming exemption from Caesar worship.[13] Threats rose from every side.[14]

The biggest problem was maintaining the purity and strength of your faith. How was one to be 'in' the world, but 'not of it' (John 17:14–16)? There were so many opportunities for compromise. Some church teachers even seemed to encourage it (Rev. 2:2,14–15,20–25). While in your heart you held deep convictions about Jesus and his teachings, everyday life would be difficult if you didn't toe the party line. Should you join in the offerings to Diana at sporting festivals, cheer at the parades that worshipped Zeus or bow down to the emperor's statue in the town square? What about trading at the market when it required burning incense to a god you didn't believe in? How were you supposed to live as a follower of Jesus in a corrupt, oppressive and abusive Roman world?

It is in this context that John's letter arrives.

02 How Did John Feel in the Dream?

Our second question of interpretation focuses on the emotions of a dream-vision. Identifying the feelings experienced in the vision as well as any shifts between them will help point to its meaning.

For John, it must have been a rollercoaster ride. We see despair, hope, shock and, finally, elation and awe . . .

We begin with the jubilation of entering God's heavenly throne-room. Imagine the joy and wonder John experienced in witnessing the grandeur and brilliance of the scene – the elders with their crowns, the winged creatures and, of course, the great throne.

The jubilation didn't last long, however, turning to weeping as the problem of the sealed scroll is announced. When no one worthy enough was found to break the seals, the realization was excruciating. A sense of hopelessness must have reverberated so deeply in John that it provoked a flood of tears. Was there no answer from heaven that would help Jesus-followers to escape the pressures of Roman rule?

Thankfully, the feeling of helplessness dissipated quickly. Someone worthy *was* found. A wave of hope and relief would have enveloped John's heart. There *was* an answer, after all. It was the 'Lion of the Tribe of Judah'.

John, of course, would be familiar with the lion imagery from the visions of the Old Covenant prophets. The Messiah was frequently spoken of as a 'lion' who would arise from the lineage of Judah (Gen. 49:9). This great kingly figure was promised as God's agent to destroy the nation's foreign oppressors and bring independence and freedom to Israel. The image of a lion conjured up ideas of a warrior in the likeness of King David (Rev. 5:5) – a great leader who would defeat the enemy by military might: 'The lion has roared – who will not fear?' (Amos 3:8). At last, it seemed, the time had come. The Lion of Judah would defeat the Eagle of Rome.[15] Behold the wrath and destructive power of the mighty Messiah!

But now comes the greatest shock of all.

Following the triumphant announcement of a candidate worthy enough to open the scroll, a small and frail lamb enters the scene. The Lion of Judah is a lamb! Somehow, the strongest creature in the animal kingdom is the weakest. Can you fathom John's confusion? *How can something so weak be so strong?*

As the scene unfolds, we can track John's changing emotions. From confusion comes elation. From understanding comes awe. Victory has been won! *It is done.* God has revealed the key to the operation of his kingdom. The appearance of the Lamb unveils the policies and strategies of his government. John is awed by the paradoxical nature of it all and joins in worship with the elders and winged creatures.

03 What Did the Symbols Mean to John and the Asian Churches?

Now we turn to the third question: the meaning of the symbols for John and the Asian churches. Remembering that the churches of Asia Minor were partly Jewish, we shouldn't be surprised that several of the images draw from Israel's story, correlating with the visions of her prophets: Isaiah, Ezekiel, Zechariah, Jeremiah and Daniel.[16] But John and the Asian churches also lived in the context of the broader Greco-Roman Empire, so we should expect to see imagery from this world too.

There are four key symbols in the opening vision of John's revelation: the throne room with twenty-four elders, the four living creatures, the scroll and the lamb.

The first symbol is the *throne room with twenty-four elders*. Throne rooms were common in the ancient world,[17] so this symbol would be familiar to the audience. But from the outset, it's clear that this throne room was not in Rome. It is the throne room of *heaven*. For John, the scene would have easily harked back to the scenes of God's throne in Isaiah (Isa. 6) and Daniel's visions (Dan. 7), with the One known as the 'Ancient of Days' seated there (Dan. 7:9).

Now we see the contrast. In the throne room of Rome, a different ruler is seated – the emperor Caesar – surrounded by his senior counsellors and attendants. The fact that they are seated on smaller thrones reinforces their leadership positions under the rule of the king. It may be no coincidence that in Emperor Domitian's time, there were *twenty-four* of them, all leading the Roman provinces on the emperor's behalf.[18] Further, it was known that when provincial leaders met with the emperor in his court, they would present a *golden crown* to him as a sign of submission and fealty.[19] Caesar was, after all, the great sovereign of the universe.

In the heavenly throne-room, there are also twenty-four leaders who pay homage to their sovereign with crowns, but these are not Roman officials. The number 24 calls up the memory of the twelve Israelite tribes of the Old Covenant and the twelve apostles of the New.[20] Together, they represent the people of God.[21] So now we have two throne rooms, two rulers and two sets of leaders in government.

The second symbol is the *four winged creatures*. As modern readers, these strange beings with a mixture of human and animal body parts appear like something out of a sci-fi movie with little precedent in our world. But in ancient times, hybrid creatures were not uncommon. For John and the Asian churches, they were reminiscent of the seraphim with six wings in Isaiah's vision (Isa. 6:2) or the cherubim with human faces in Ezekiel's (Ezek. 1:5–14). Likely, the creatures in the throne room represent *all* of creation – both human and animal. They reinforce the message that the whole of creation bows to God's rule![22]

The third symbol is the all-important *scroll*. The scroll lies in God's *right* hand, the hand of power and authority. It is secured with seven wax seals to shield its contents from unworthy eyes. In the Roman world, the image of a scroll was often associated with emperors. Archaeologists have even discovered statues of Domitian holding a scroll in his right hand![23] What's more, the scroll in John's vision is *sealed*, guaranteeing its authenticity. Only an authorized person could open it and carry out its instructions. So, what does the scroll represent? Perhaps it is some sort of legal document – a policy or constitution, or maybe a plan for the future to be outworked by the sovereign.[24] Clearly, its contents are crucial in understanding the ways of God's government.

To receive the Spirit's message, the scroll must be opened. This was God's revelation for the early church. Its contents would remind them of Jesus and how his message applied to their lives (John 14:26; 16:13).

Finally, we come to the fourth and most important symbol in this vision: *the lamb*. As noted, this image would have shocked its first audience, who were anticipating a lion. Yet there is more to this symbol than just the promise of a Jewish messiah. In the context of Rome, the lion represented *conquest*. This makes the imagery of the scene even more poignant. In the place of a powerful and ferocious figure, we have a small and frail lamb.

The lamb symbol harks back centuries earlier to the time of the Passover when the Jews were about to begin their exodus from Egypt (Exod. 12). Back then, a lamb gave its life in each Israelite household so that the people could be saved from death and reconciled to God. It is a small, vulnerable creature associated with submission, sacrifice and suffering, but never with power (Isa. 53:7). Yet the lamb in the vision is also unusual in that it has seven eyes – a symbol of perfect *vision* – and seven horns – a symbol of perfect *strength*. Here we have the truth that encapsulates the entire scene. The quality of perceived weakness is the lamb's greatest strength!

When the lamb finally appears, the elders and winged creatures declare its worthiness to open the scroll. The lamb alone brings salvation to 'every tribe and language and people and nation' (Rev. 5:9–10). Now we see that the lamb who brought salvation to the Jews has brought salvation to everyone.

Of course, this symbol represents Jesus, the *Lamb of God*, given for the sin of the world, the one who 'humbled himself by becoming obedient to death – even death on a cross!' (Phil. 2:8). In Jesus' crucifixion, we see God's ultimate way of rule in heaven's government: self-sacrificial love.

The Key to God's Kingdom

The scene of the sacrificial lamb in God's throne room is the basis for deciphering the meaning of the remaining visions in

John's Vision of the Heavenly Government

Revelation. The Lamb alone unlocks the seals and reveals God's ways. Answering our three interpretative questions brings clarity and understanding to John's prophetic message.

The people of the seven Asian churches had experienced one government. They had seen the ways of the Roman Empire with its abuse of power, wealth and fame. They had witnessed how the king on his earthly throne exercised authority through coercion, exploitation and violence. Now they are beginning to see the ways of another kingdom with a different throne and a different king. They see how a weak-looking lamb contains the power of a conquering lion through the policy of self-sacrificial love. No wonder the twenty-four leaders and winged creatures around the throne erupted in wonder and praise!

The lamb on the throne was the basis for all God's governmental operations, but there was more to see. In the next chapter, we apply our interpretative skills to three additional visions in order to understand the full message of the scroll. We will see what happens when two powerful governments clash and a seven-headed dragon arises to wage war against the Lamb!

More on Symbols (1): The Dragon and a Pregnant Woman

It's difficult to imagine a more disturbing scene. As the lamb begins to break the seals on the scroll, all hell breaks loose. One by one, four colourful horsemen appear with devastating effect. They come with famine, foreign invasion, natural disasters, war and death, and lots of it.

This set of visions in John's revelation appears in terrible contrast to the scene of the throne room before it. Unlike the heartening introduction to God's way of the Lamb, the next few scenes in John's visions project all the ills of humanity onto the visionary screen. There is no holding back. For the early church, it must have felt like the end of the world as all of life's suffering is depicted in graphic detail.

As we've seen, the book of Revelation provides us with the most comprehensive example of symbolic dream-visions in the early church. It offers us an opportunity to learn from the God-conversations of that time and, in doing so, develop the interpretative skills for the God-conversations of our own.

More on Symbols (1): The Dragon and the Pregnant Woman 153

In this chapter and the next, we explore the nature of symbols in greater depth, drawing from several additional scenes in John's visions. Here, we examine three: the seven sets of seals, trumpets and bowls; the partying crowd; and a woman clothed with the sun. Together they point to the implications of the Lamb's reign from the heavenly throne on the earth, where everything is not as it seems.

The three scenes demonstrate how numbers can act as symbols, how two different symbols can carry the same meaning, and how symbols can be mixed and matched together to reinforce a single message. We also learn that symbols can be used to depict spiritual realities and hence don't always follow the rules of the natural world.

Seven Seals, Seven Trumpets and Seven Bowls

Our vision begins with the opening of the scroll's seven seals (Rev. 6). Later we learn about seven trumpets (Rev. 8 – 11) and seven bowls (Rev. 16). Catastrophe follows the mention of each one. Whenever a seal is opened, a trumpet is sounded or a bowl is emptied, there is violence, famine and death. Then, in a horrifying twist, we notice that the drama increases with each round of symbols. The trumpets bear worse atrocities than the seals, and the bowls bear worse atrocities than the trumpets. The wars get bloodier, the number of deaths escalate, and the area of destroyed land expands at a staggering rate. The message repeats itself over and over in relentless waves.[1]

What is happening here? What is the significance of the seven seals, seven trumpets and seven bowls?

You will notice that the number 7 connects all three symbols. The use of symbolic numbers is common in Revelation, with 7 being one of the most frequent. For example, John's visions began with *seven* churches and *seven* lampstands. Then we see the lamb has *seven* eyes and *seven* horns. Later, there are *seven* kings, a beast with *seven* heads, *seven* angels and *seven* plagues, and so on.

Although numbers do not always carry symbolic meaning in dream-visions, in this case they clearly do. In the ancient world, 7 was associated with perfection and completion. The number itself points to a bigger story. The emphasis is not so much on the particulars of each seal, trumpet or bowl as on their overall message.

The meaning of the seals, trumpets and bowls becomes clearer when we remind ourselves of the first-century setting. All these dreadful sufferings are the product of Rome's earthly rule and, more broadly, sin and evil. They are vivid depictions of the outcomes of imperial idolatry, oppression and abuse.[2] We see what happens when God's grace is lifted and human selfishness reigns unchecked. Sin brings its own judgement.

This is probably how it would have felt for the first audience. The events surrounding the opening of the seals easily correlate with the disasters that occurred under the rule of the seven prominent emperors following the time of Christ.[3] For example, at the second seal's opening, the appearance of a fiery red horse taking peace from the earth (Rev. 6:3–4) would have likely conjured up memories of the reign of the mad and unpredictable emperor Caligula in 37–40 CE.[4] The famine wrought by the opening of the third seal would have reminded the audience of the heart-wrenching famines under Claudius in 41–54 CE.[5] Though we cannot pinpoint the specifics, altogether the seals describe a world of pain and suffering familiar to those living in the kingdom of Rome.

We see here how different symbols can be used to bear the same meaning. In this case, the seals, trumpets and bowls all share the common theme of disaster.[6] Their repetition brings emphasis to the message as well as adding a range of dimensions to it. You may have seen this dynamic in your own experience. Different symbols can be connected by a common thread. In my own life, for example, God's promises have been variously described as a 'suitcase' I need to carry, a 'treasure' I need to protect and a 'gift' I need to wait patiently for at Christmas time. The power of symbolic language lies in its ability to depict a message from a variety of angles.

In the case of John's visions, the seals carry the dimension of providing context for the scroll's message, the trumpets point to the announcement of a warning and call to action, and the bowls communicate the idea that sin builds up and eventually overflows with devastating effect. The question becomes: how does all this pain and suffering fit into God's kingdom plan? How were God's people to understand the dark side of life under Rome and, more importantly, how were they to respond?

The Partying Crowd

In the midst of all the devastation wrought by the opening of the seals, John's vision shifts. He sees a great crowd of 144,000 in celebration (Rev. 7), followed by a countless multitude dressed in white robes and waving palm fronds. It's a welcome relief after all the violence and death. Who are these people and why are they partying?

The symbols in the vision give us our answer. To begin with, the men and women in the multitude are wearing *white robes*. This type of dress was often used in the first century to depict victory. White robes are also worn in baptism and carry the connotation of purity. Here, they indicate that the crowd has overcome the trials and suffering of the world. Even when faced with the worst the world can bring, the people have not faltered. They have 'come out of the great tribulation', having 'washed their robes and made them white in the blood of the Lamb' (Rev. 7:14). Of course, the reason for their joy is the Lamb and his victory. As the Lamb's followers, they are sealed by him and therefore share in his triumph.[7]

The number of the crowd first introduced in the scene[8] – 144,000 – tells us who these people are. We've already seen how numbers act symbolically with the use of 7; here we see the significance of 12. The number 12 is an important symbol in the history of Israel, with the twelve tribes of the 'Old Israel' and the twelve apostles of the 'New Israel' (see also Rev. 12:12,14). Multiplied together, we have 144. This number is then multiplied by 1,000, one of the largest numerical units in the Bible. Overall, the number points to the identity of the crowd as the completed people of God and then, of course, its enormous size. This mighty group comprises those in the lineage of Israel as well as those 'from every nation, tribe, people and language' (Rev. 7:9).[9] Together they are victorious over the challenges of the first-century world.

More on Symbols (1): The Dragon and the Pregnant Woman

We've seen how the symbols of the seals, trumpets and bowls reveal the ills of sin in the human kingdom. When left unchecked, evil brings untold suffering and, ultimately, its own judgement. We've also witnessed God's great and faithful crowd who follow the Lamb. All is set for the answer to the burning question: *how* do God's people overcome in a kingdom where sin and idolatry is the motivation for rule?

The Woman with Twelve Stars

Our answer comes in a third scene. A pregnant woman appears in startling array. She is clothed with the sun, has the moon at her feet, and wears a crown of twelve gold stars on her head (Rev. 12). Her brilliance and light fill the atmosphere. She is also in the final stages of labour. It's a moment of great hope and expectation.

Suddenly a ghastly beast appears. As it unfurls its enormous body, we see a ferocious red dragon complete with seven heads and ten horns. On each of its seven heads is a crown. It hovers ominously over the woman, its back arching and tail swaying vigorously in threat. It waits for the woman to give birth so as to devour the child.

But the dragon has no hope of victory against the power of God. When the baby is born, the mother and child are dramatically rescued and carried to safety.

In response, the dragon explodes in fury. A mighty war breaks out between the dragon and the angel Michael and their armies.

Thankfully, the seven-headed dragon is defeated. It is thrown down and hurled to the earth.

* * *

We have seen God's throne room, devastation on the earth and the victory of God's people. Now we see the key issue behind it all. In this vision, the curtain opens further to reveal a scene depicting a battle between two players: a dragon and a pregnant woman. We see that underlying the everyday activities of the natural world are spiritual realities that drive and shape them. God was calling his people to look *behind* the scenes of their earthly problem so they could discover the heavenly solution. This was an opportunity to see life as God saw it.

In truth, there was a war in the spiritual realms. The battle of the dragon and the pregnant woman revealed a conflict between two kingdoms. In one corner was the human kingdom where evil and sin reigned; in the other was God's kingdom where the ways of the Lamb reigned.

To better understand this cosmic war, we must understand what the woman and the dragon meant for the first-century audience. To our minds, it might evoke the scene of the Virgin Mary and her son Jesus, with King Herod trying to kill him. But in John's time, another tale of a woman and a dragon probably came to mind. This popular Greek myth told of the god Zeus and a woman named Leto. In the story, Leto had sex with Zeus and became pregnant. Zeus's wife was furious and sent a snake-like dragon to watch over Leto and devour her offspring. As they were about to be consumed, Zeus intervened and rescued them.[10]

Sound familiar? The main difference, of course, is the identity of the mother and child. In John's version, the pregnant woman has a crown of *twelve* stars on her head, an indicator that she represents God's people – the twelve tribes of Israel – who 'gave birth' to the promised child, Jesus. The woman is also clothed with stars, sun and moon, representing Israel's call to bring God's plan to all creation.[11]

Hence the scene zooms in on the heart of the cosmic battle – Jesus' birth – and the opposition it provoked. There is no ambiguity about the identity of the dragon. John tells us that the dragon is 'that ancient snake called the devil, or Satan, who leads the whole world astray' (Rev. 12:9). In fact, the dragon was a well-known symbol in the ancient world. The Babylonians called him 'Tiamat'; the Hebrews, 'Leviathan'; and the Greeks, 'Python'.[12] All understood the dragon to represent *chaos* and *evil*.

John's vision of the pregnant woman with twelve stars shows that from the outset, God's arch-enemy was bent on destroying the Messiah. The good news is that Satan's cause was lost – Jesus is safe, and the dragon has been hurled down. In the heavenly realms, the battle *has been won*! (Rev. 12:10–11).

Yet sadly, this is not the end of the scene. Even though the baby has escaped, and the spiritual war is won, we now see the dragon pursuing the woman and the rest of her offspring (Rev. 12:13,17). These are the people of God on earth who 'keep the testimony of Jesus'. The war is now on earth and all are under attack!

* * *

Once again, we see the power of symbols to communicate a message – in this case an alternative reality behind the scenes of the natural world. Symbols are cleverly mixed and matched to reinforce the message. Cultural mythologies and everyday items are incorporated into the plotlines. Numbers too become part of the story.

John's visions of the seven sets of seals, trumpets and bowls, the partying crowd and the pregnant woman's battle with the dragon provide the first-century audience with a bigger picture. Having understood the defining feature of God's kingdom through the way of the Lamb, they learn how this changes the way they see the world around them.

Now they understand the ultimate cause of their challenges on earth. Suffering comes as the inevitable outcome of a world that is orientated towards sin and selfishness and idolizes the gods of Rome. Behind the pain of this life is an enemy who strikes at the heart of those who follow the Lamb. He pursued Jesus and is now pursuing the church. Yes, there was victory in heaven, but now there is a battle on earth and, like it or not, the church is in the middle of it. The question is: how are they to fight?

More on Symbols (2): Two Kingdoms at War

The battle in the heavens may have been won, but now the seven-headed dragon appears on the earth. He is angry and he is not alone (Rev. 13). From the sea, a second beast emerges. Like the dragon, it has seven heads, as well as the body of a leopard, the feet of a bear and the mouth of a lion. It gains its power and authority from the dragon. But there's more. A third beast emerges, this time from the land. It has two horns, speaks like a dragon and calls down fire from the heavens. It too derives its power from the dragon.

A trinity of monstrous beasts now ravages the earth. Their mouths are full of abusive and blasphemous threats, and they attack with coercive and destructive power. Their goal? To deceive all the world's people and, ultimately, overcome the 'offspring' of the woman, the church.

John could have been forgiven for thinking the war was over with the dragon's defeat in his earlier vision. After all, the woman and her baby were safe. But in this ghastly scene, John is introduced to a new phase in the battle. He is about to discover more about the war on earth, including the opposition's strategy and the type of weaponry the church was to wield in response. He would learn, too, of all that was at stake. Only after understanding the true nature of the battle would John and the seven churches be equipped to fight it.

In this chapter, we build on our understanding of symbols by reflecting on some of the final scenes in Revelation: the dragon's sidekicks, two beautiful women, two types of weaponry and two great cities. These visions provide us with more examples of how symbolic language works in dream-visions. We learn how symbols can have collective meaning for a culture and how that meaning can change over time. We also see several more cases of symbols used in contrast in order to accentuate a message.

The Dragon's Sidekicks

The dragon and his sidekicks are prominent symbols in the battle on earth. We know who the dragon represents, but who are his associates?

The distinctive features of the two beasts give us a clue. To begin with, the sea-beast has seven heads like the dragon, and bears seven crowns and ten horns. Locals would immediately understand the seven heads to be a reference to the Roman Empire and its kings. Everyone knew that Rome was the city built on seven hills.[1] We also know that there were also seven prominent emperors between the time of Christ and John, each bearing the authority of a crown and the strength of a horn.

More on Symbols (2): Two Kingdoms at War 163

So we see that the symbols of the dragon and sea-beast are a pointed reference to the Roman Empire and, more broadly, the values and ideals that perpetuate its reign. The connection is made even more explicit with the descriptions of the sea-beast's body parts – those of a lion, bear and leopard. First hearers would have immediately recalled the beast imagery in Daniel's writings, which were immensely popular at the time. In an uncanny parallel, Daniel's vision also features a lion, bear and leopard, and a beast with ten horns (Dan. 7:3–7). In Daniel's day, these beasts represented the ruling empires of Israel's history up until the time of Jesus – from the Babylonians to the Medes to the Persians and the Greeks.[2] It is no coincidence that in John's vision, the sea-beast combines all the features of Daniel's beasts to depict one great anti-Jesus empire.[3]

In the symbolism of the beasts, we are reminded of the need to consider the setting of a vision in order to realize its meaning. To our modern minds, the imagery of the beasts appears odd and unfamiliar, almost fanciful. Images like these are unlikely to appear in our dreams unless we've been watching a lot of sci-fi![4]

I remember several years ago visiting a museum featuring exhibits from centuries before Christ. Suddenly I was immersed in the world of the ancients. All around me were statues of hybrid creatures – animals with human faces and dragons with human bodies. Through my twenty-first-century eyes, they seemed peculiar and surreal, but this was the norm in the ancient world. Hybrid creatures represented spiritual beings and were as common as billboards on the highway. Think of the Great Sphinx in Egypt or the gargoyles adorning medieval cathedrals. In our day, spiritual beings are more likely to be depicted as smiling cherubim floating on clouds, or wisps of smoke passing through walls and messing with light bulbs. Here we see how the meaning of symbols can be shared by an entire culture, and that over time the meaning may shift until the symbols are almost unrecognizable. Without knowing the setting of the dream-vision, it is too easy to overlay one cultural perspective with another and, in doing so, distort its meaning.

After meeting the two beastly sidekicks, John and the Asian churches begin to learn of their ways. Both derive their power and authority from the dragon. Both evoke wonder and awe among the people, and both lead them to *worship the dragon* (Rev. 13:4). They are the dragon's henchmen who wage war against God's people by making claims about *who* is worthy to sit on the throne (Rev. 13:6–7).[5]

The connection between the spiritual and natural worlds now began to crystallize for the early Christians. As they learned about the beasts' activities, they were confronted with the implications for their everyday lives. With fresh perspective, they could realize the significance of the emperor's demands to be referred to as 'Lord', 'Son of God' and 'Saviour', and why his image on Roman coins was made to resemble those of the gods. In a new light, they could see the motivation behind the provincial governors who competed with one another to build the largest temples and curry the emperor's favour. And with renewed understanding, they could see the forces behind the trade guilds forcing customers to mark their foreheads and offer sacrifices to the emperor as a precondition for buying and selling.[6]

The message is now plain. All of this was the work of the sea-beast and the land-beast. Together they functioned at the heart of the human empire, vying for sovereignty above the one true

God and employing methods that were the antithesis of God's rule. Behind the pressure to burn incense at the marketplace, pay homage to the Roman gods at festivals and bow down to the emperor's statue in the town square was Satan, the great dragon and enemy of God who ruled victorious whenever a human emperor ruled on the throne of people's hearts. The tactics behind the cosmic war were becoming clearer and clearer.

Two Beautiful Women

In John's visions, we see the truth behind the workings of the human empire. Whenever the ways of Rome were exalted above the true King of Kings, the dragon reigned and evil proliferated. But if the ways of the enemy were so dehumanizing and oppressive, why would anyone adopt them?

The answer lies in our next vision. From two ugly beasts, we turn to two beautiful women. The first woman rides the seven-headed beast (Rev. 17). She is devastatingly attractive, lavishly dressed in purple and red, and bedecked with glittering jewels. Heads turn as she passes by.

In her hand, the woman carries a golden cup. She drinks freely, filling her belly with its intoxicating delights. Then she offers her cup to kings and all those around. The people drink deeply and become wildly intoxicated.

But then the scene turns, and the contents of the cup are exposed. Now we see that the cup overflows with *filth*. It contains the blood of those who have given their lives because of their faith in Jesus. When the people drink it, they fall sick from its toxicity.

Who is this woman dressed in purple and red? We know she is aligned to the beast since she rides the seven-headed dragon,[7] but unlike the beast, she is not known for her ferocity or violence. Instead, her pull lies in her appearance. She wears purple and red, the colours of luxury and status. Costly jewels speak of her bountiful wealth. The woman reflects the ways of the empire – so attractive and seductive that they capture the hearts of Rome's leaders and her people.

At first, the woman's delights are intoxicating, filling her lovers with ecstasy and joy. But the woman is a *courtesan* – a prostitute, who uses others for her own ends. With her wealth and beauty, she lures people into a system that controls, enslaves and exploits in order to enhance its own success. One shouldn't be surprised, given that the woman rides on the back of the dragon. She embodies a system where its citizens are used and spat out for the might of Rome. Those who refuse to condescend to her seductions are killed for their stance. All suffer from drinking the wine of her adulteries.

The significance of the prostitute symbol is made even clearer when juxtaposed with the symbol of the second woman (Rev. 19). This woman is also beautiful, but her attractiveness derives from a different source. She is clothed in fine white linen. This woman is a bride.

The imagery of the two women provides a stunning contrast. Compare the heart of a bride with the heart of a prostitute. To 'prostitute' oneself is to use one's talents for disrespectful or unworthy ends. In this scene, the prostitute acts to *get* something out of you, while the bride acts to *give* something to you. One is motivated by self-gain, the other by love. Side by side, the two symbols provide a comparison that cuts to the very heart. Their clever pairing highlights their differences and reveals their true meaning.

Now our focus turns to the bride. How different she is! Unlike the prostitute whose beauty lies in her outer appearance, the bride's attractiveness lies in her inner deeds. She is adorned with kindness, generosity and grace. All those around receive from her goodness. And of course, she is dressed for a wedding. Her ways are deeply wedded to the groom.

The two kingdoms could not be more different. The kingdom of God is ruled by the ways of a self-sacrificial lamb. It is a bride motivated by love, grace and generosity. The kingdom of Satan is led by a fire-breathing beast. It exerts power through greed and exploitation. It is a prostitute who parades beauty and joy but brings sickness and death to all those who receive from it. Why were the ways of the dragon so successful? Because of their seductive power. Because of the pleasures they brought and the delights they promised. The dragon's ways were powerful because they felt so good – at first. But in the end, they led to degradation and death.

Two Types of Weaponry

Armed with a revelation of the Enemy's strategies, the early Christians had the advantage, but they were still confronted with their earthly reality. Even with a true perspective, they were still a weak and insignificant minority pitted against the might of the Roman system. If the weapons of the human kingdom were abuse, violence and oppression, what weapons was the church to use? The Enemy's devices seemed overwhelmingly powerful. Rome's strength was on display every time you turned over a Roman coin,[8] passed a centurion on the street, or heard of an accused traitor being executed. Rome's authority was unsurpassed. Who could stand against it?

Another vision points the way forward. In the scene, a rider on a white horse enters centre stage (Rev. 19:11–16). His eyes are blazing with fire, and he has several crowns on his head. He wears a robe dipped in blood and carries a sword in his mouth. Written on his thigh is the name 'King of Kings and Lord of Lords'. Following behind him is a great army riding white horses and dressed in white linen. We've met this crowd before. We know who they are and who they follow.

Now the dragon responds. He gathers his armies together. Death and destruction linger in the air. The scene is set for a great cosmic war.

But suddenly, the battle is over.

The dragon is captured and later annihilated (Rev. 20:10). His minions are thrown into a lake of sulphur, and his army is destroyed by the sword in the rider's mouth (Rev. 19:20–21).

It's a dramatic plot twist. There is no battle. The great cosmic war is won. Victory belongs to the rider with blood on his robe. The One who appeared as a lamb so pitifully weak against the dragon's might is now leader of the conquering army. The dragon, his beasts and followers are all overcome.

The vision of the rider on the white horse is a definitive moment in the story. It presents God's battle strategy and how the followers of Jesus can overcome evil as members of God's army. Having sealed their allegiance to God (Rev. 7), God's people can only defeat the dragon and his beasts by way of the Lamb. The battle is fought with uncompromising faithfulness to the Lamb's ways, no matter the cost (Rev. 12:11).

Note how the scene also compares the weaponry of God's kingdom with that of the human kingdom. Like the Roman emperor who was often depicted on a warhorse, Jesus too is riding a horse. Both are seen as military leaders leading their army into battle.[9] But note the difference – the blood on Jesus' robe is his own, and he doesn't carry a sword in his hand. Instead, the sword is *in his mouth*. It is the message of good news – the 'Word of God' (Rev. 19:13) – that remains God's greatest weapon. The message of God's love for humanity and his willingness to lay down his life is more powerful than any human force. The use of coercion, violence and exploitation falls away to nothing in the light of the Lamb's power. The way of the Lamb triumphs over the way of the beast! (Rev. 17:14).

The meaning of the rider's weaponry was a radical one for the early church. It was the complete undoing of everything humanity stood for. Where Rome pursued victory through wealth and status, the Lamb pursued victory through sacrifice and humility. Where Rome paraded strength through violence and oppression, the Lamb pursued strength through self-sacrificial love. Mercy and grace became the driving motivation, with complete surrender of one's life for the sake of others the goal. This was loving your neighbour and your enemy at a level not seen in the Roman world. Such is the way of the Lamb – God's ultimate weapon and the power that defeats all human powers.

It is an utter reversal of every method that pushes its way through, stands on the heads of others, steals and lies to get its own way; that competes to be the first, the greatest and the best and doesn't care about any collateral damage.

The implications of the vision had practical consequences for God's people. How were they to fight evil in the world around them? How were they to escape the oppression of Roman rule? They were to remain faithful to Jesus, no matter the outcome. They were to follow the way of the Lamb. They were to clothe themselves with white robes of purity and righteous acts (Rev. 19:8). They were to proclaim the good news of Jesus with their mouths and by the 'word of their testimony' (Rev. 12:11,17). They were to love their enemies even if it meant laying down their lives for them.

Two Great Cities

The beauty of symbolic language lies in its potential to communicate from multiple angles. We have seen the operation of two kingdoms, and how they contrast with each other via the imagery of a dragon and a lamb, a sword held in the hand rather than the mouth, and a prostitute and a bride. One final pair of images remains. These symbols reveal the finale of the cosmic battle and all that God's people were fighting for.

Our last symbol is a city. Two are presented in John's visions: the city of Babylon and the city of Jerusalem. Babylon is aligned to the prostitute (Rev. 17 – 18) and Jerusalem is aligned to the bride (Rev. 21 – 22).[10]

More on Symbols (2): Two Kingdoms at War

We understand the symbolic meaning of these two cities when we consider the characteristics of their reign. Jerusalem of the first century was the home of God's people Israel. It was also understood to be the place where God's presence dwelt.

If we know our biblical history, we will also be familiar with the city of Babylon. Babylon was the capital of one of the world's greatest empires, famous for its imperial grandeur and military prowess. But Babylon was also known for its violence, the brutal subjugation of its enemies and neglect of the poor. More particularly, it was known for the way it destroyed Jerusalem in the sixth century BCE and sent God's people into exile.

We can see, then, how a first-century Jewish audience would have made the correlation between sixth-century BCE Babylon and first-century CE Rome. Like the powerful regime of old, Rome extended its territory by violence, force and plundering. The meaning of the first city, Babylon, is clear.

But what of the second city?

The second city is presented as the new 'Jerusalem'. It comes down to earth from heaven and is built with twelve gates and twelve foundations. It's an unusual city in that it is defined by what it *doesn't have*. There is no sun or moon lighting its paths. There is no temple and no sea, and its gates are never closed.

What kind of city is this? What does it represent?

Whenever we see two different symbols paired together, the key to their interpretation lies in how their features are held in contrast. As in the case of the two beautiful women and the two types of weaponry, we see that the two cities are vastly different from each other – but how?

To begin with, the new Jerusalem has no sea. In the ancient world, the sea was a symbol of chaos and evil. Without a sea, this city has no sin and death. Neither does it have lighting, because it has *no night*. The darkness of sadness isn't present here. The city is also without a temple. God's presence is no longer walled in by stone and timber – it permeates the entire precinct.

Even more bizarrely for an ancient city, the gates of the new Jerusalem are always *open*. Everyone is invited to enter, no matter who they are! The city is unique because the culture of the Lamb is present and the way of the beast is not. Its inhabitants have been washed clean, and in them nothing impure or shameful is found (Rev. 21:27; 22:14–15). This is a place of peace, love and light. It is the kingdom of God operating in all its fullness and beauty. This is what the church was fighting for. God's *kingdom come* – his will being done on earth, just as it is in heaven.

* * *

Perhaps now you can more fully imagine how it felt to be a member of the first-century Asian church hearing about John's visions for the first time. There was an unveiling of truth and reality, a presentation of divine strategy and, ultimately, a promise of hope and life. Here is the power of a God-dream. Using the dynamic of contrast and a colourful array of symbols from the first-century world, Holy Spirit was able to reinforce God's message to his people over and over again. The imagery of beasts, women, cities, armies, weaponry and a victorious rider are mixed and matched to send a clarion call as relevant to the church today as it was in the first century.

More on Symbols (2): Two Kingdoms at War

The people of God knew they were fighting a cosmic battle against the powers of darkness. Knowing that victory was assured through the Lamb, they understood their ultimate goal – a dwelling place on earth where everyone is welcome; where sin, evil and injustice is absent; and where the presence of God isn't limited to a building, city or nation. It is the living reality of a kingdom that exists whenever the Lamb reigns on the throne of people's hearts. This was the mission of God's people, the church. They were to follow the ways of the Lamb and, in doing so, bring God's kingdom from heaven to earth.

The battle lines had been drawn, the weapons revealed and the goal presented. This is the message of the scroll, vividly communicated in a collection of powerful symbols. The revelation was clear to its audience. The next question, then, is: how did they know it was from God?

How Do You Know It's a God-Dream?

If you were to open the Bible today, you would find the book of Revelation firmly fixed in its pages. But it hasn't always been that way. Not everyone thought that John's weird and wonderful depictions of beasts, dragons and attractive women was relevant for the church of all time. In fact, this little book with a big message has been one of the most controversial pieces of writing in church history. When the canon of the Scriptures was closed in the late fourth century, it was the last text to be included, and only then with the proviso that it *not* be used to speculate over future events.[1] During the sixteenth-century Reformation, Martin Luther argued for Revelation to be completely ousted from the Bible, and today the Eastern Orthodox Church does not include it in its public liturgy. Its unusual style meant that not everyone thought it was of God.

On the other hand, we know that the early Christians accepted John's visions with enthusiasm and deference. They believed his experiences to be divinely inspired, and treated them as such. The question is: how did John and the Asian churches know they were from God? Like us, the characters of the New

Testament were subject to the fog of human influence, emotion and bias. Like us, they could have got it wrong.

What's more, the implications of Revelation's message were dire. It was no small thing to stay faithful to the Lamb in the face of Roman power. As we've seen, Antipas had already paid the highest price in Pergamum, and John's prophetic message hinted at worse to come (Rev. 2:10). This was a matter of life and death. While the early Asian churches might have trusted John's leadership, there was still a need for testing.

In the previous chapters, we applied the first three questions of the God Dreams framework to the message of John's dream-visions. In this chapter, we apply the fourth question: *Where did the dream-vision come from?* Even though we already know the answer since the early church discerned John's experiences to be from God and later canonized his writings about them as Scripture, our discussion will help us identify the source of our own visionary experiences.

Testing the Source

Our starting point for identifying a God-dream is to acknowledge that, in the same way that not every waking thought is from God, not every dream is from God. Indeed, most of them are not! As noted (Chapter 5), dreams arise from three possible sources: natural dreams that are reflections of ourselves, spiritual dreams that arise from other spirits, and God-dreams that act as Jesus' continuing voice.

On a practical level, it is important to remember that the majority of our dreams are *natural*. We dream on average six to seven times a night and most of these reflect the recent happenings in our lives. So, if our dream just rehashes what we were thinking about the day or week before, it's likely to be a natural dream.

It's also helpful to know that a God-dream does not always feel that different from a natural dream. Unless it is an external experience (the exception rather than the rule), there is not usually some sort of hallowed glow or shimmery presence when you wake up.

Discerning God's voice is often a challenge, but it seems particularly problematic in the area of dream-visions. Perhaps this is due to the creative nature of imagery and the fact that our imaginations seem to run wild while we sleep.

Our main difficulty lies in separating the natural thoughts from the spiritual. Even the biblical characters experienced this. The prophet Jeremiah, for example, clashed with a group of prophets just prior to the Babylonian exile. These prophets had claimed that it was God speaking to them in dreams, but Jeremiah discerned that their dreams had come from 'their own minds' (Jer. 23:25–29). Tragically, the people followed the message of the false prophets rather than Jeremiah's and were led astray as a result (Jer. 23:32).

This is the reason Scripture tells us that every claim to revelation must be put to the test (1 John 4:1). As the apostle Paul taught, we don't see clearly (1 Cor. 13:9–12) – and even more so in our dreams! Testing is a safety measure that keeps us from confusion and deception. It is a crucial part of the interpretative process. Once we have identified the source, we can be confident in our response.

04 Where Did John's Dream-Vision Come From?

So let's return to the source of John's dream-visions. How did John and the seven churches know they were from God?

In Chapter 7, we identified three questions of discernment based on Peter's vision of an unappetizing lunch:

1. Would Jesus say this?
2. Is someone else saying this?
3. Are spiritual signs following this?

Here we unpack the three test questions in more detail and show how they apply to John's visions in Revelation.

1. Would Jesus Say This?

The first and most important test question to ask of our spiritual experiences is: 'Would Jesus say this?'

We know that Jesus sent the Holy Spirit as his continuing voice, reminding us of all that he had established (John 14:26) and then applying those truths to 'what [was] yet to come' (John 16:13). Therefore, everything the Spirit says today will be consistent with the way God has already spoken in Jesus, God's living Word in the flesh.

This truth frames our understanding of the messaging in God-dreams. The Holy Spirit speaks to continue God's ministry and mission on earth. An authentic God-dream will therefore call us to follow the ways of the Lamb and partner with him in bringing God's kingdom down from heaven to earth. We will be reminded of Jesus and led to apply his truths to our individual situations. The goal will be to cultivate a relationship with the One whose character and nature is most fully seen in Jesus.

Remembering that God-dreams will be in keeping with our walk with God, it is wise to start with our individual situation and reflect on what God has been speaking about lately. You might consider the prayers you've been praying and the situation you find yourself in. It is about recognizing the voice of the One you know and seeing whether it is consistent with your ongoing conversations with God. The voice of God in our dream-visions is the same voice we hear when we are stirred by a passage of Scripture, or when our heart leaps at an accurate prophecy, or our thoughts are arrested by the words of a sermon. Ultimately, it will reflect the teachings and actions of Jesus. When it's God's message, the answer to our first test question will always be: 'Yes, Jesus would say this.'

Would Jesus speak of a lamb with a lion's power?

Let's now apply this first question of discernment to the dream-visions of Revelation. Would Jesus speak of a lamb with a lion's power?

When we place ourselves in the position of the first-century church, we see that the message of John's visions was a radical departure from the accepted way of life under Roman rule. The early Christians knew about the life of Jesus from a generation or two before, but now they were being called to apply his example to their situation. How would they know that the symbols of the beasts, women and cities really depicted the spiritual reality behind the scenes? How were they to be sure that God's way was to love Roman soldiers rather than take up arms against them? Should they really refuse to worship the emperor, and suffer from not being able to trade at the marketplace? What if they were required to choose their faith over their lives?

The message of Revelation would have been even more challenging to hear given Israel's history. As with other cultures in the ancient world, the Jewish way to fight political oppression was largely through a holy war led by a militaristic-type messiah. The Jews still celebrated David who had led Israel into battle with the Philistines and, later, Judas Maccabeus who had revolted against the Seleucids with swords and bows. More recently, the Jewish Zealots had picked up the patriotic charge by calling their countrymen to take up the sword against the Romans to retake the city of Jerusalem. The way had nearly always been through a lion rather than a lamb.

So, returning to our question, would Jesus speak of a lamb as the way to victory? The answer of course is 'Yes'. With his life and teachings alive in their memories, the early Christians had a clear reference point for the lamb who bore the power of a lion. The way of God's kingdom as depicted in Revelation is entirely consistent with the teachings and practices of Jesus. This is the one who preached about loving your enemies, doing good to those who hurt you, going the extra mile for those who cause offence and even dying for those who want to kill you. The Jesus of history is entirely consistent with the rider who entered the battle with his own blood on his robe (Rev. 19:13), whose sword was in his mouth rather than his hand (Rev. 19:15) and who rode a white horse of peace rather than the red horse of war (Rev. 6:3–4). Jesus hasn't changed. Self-sacrificial love is and always has been God's most potent weapon for overcoming evil. Jesus' resurrection proved it. His call to take up our own crosses reinforces it (Matt. 16:24).

The question 'Would Jesus say this?' is the foundational test of any God-dream. As in John's revelation, true Spirit experiences will always reflect the heart of Jesus and lead us to follow in his steps. This is the most important criterion for identifying God-dreams. We must get to know Jesus and become familiar with his life and teachings if we are to discern the Spirit in our dreams. For as the angel of Revelation said: 'it is the Spirit of prophecy who bears testimony to Jesus' (Rev. 19:10).

2. Is Someone Else Saying This?

Our second question for discerning the source of a dream-visions asks: 'Is someone else saying this?'

The beauty of the New Covenant is that the Spirit was given to *all* people – 'young and old' and 'sons and daughters' (see Acts 2:16–17). This universal outpouring means that God can speak the same message to more than one person and, in doing so, provide a corroborating witness. We saw this pattern in the testimony of Peter and Cornelius. At around the same time as Peter was having his vision of an unappetizing lunch, Cornelius was hearing from God too. The Spirit brought them together and they realized that God was speaking twice.

This dynamic is common in the church today. In one case, a friend of mine had been struggling to hear God's voice, so I encouraged him to be open to God-dreams. A month or so later, he phoned with the news. He'd had a God-dream! In the dream, he had seen himself driving up a mountain when a storm hit, making the road treacherous and difficult. But he persevered, continuing to climb higher and higher up the mountain. When he finally reached the summit, he discovered a hospital.

My friend related to the storm in his life, the dark and unpredictable journey calling him to persevere, and then the hospital at the end. After a difficult season, God had led him into a time of healing. The dream was on point in every way. When my friend's wife woke up, he eagerly shared his dream with her. As he told her about the mountain, the storm and the hospital, she gasped in astonishment: 'I've just had the same dream!'

How wonderful to know that the Spirit helps us recognize God's voice by providing a witness to his messages! There is safety in numbers! But what about the visions of John in the early church? How did God confirm his message to John through the voice of others? While it's not possible to completely re-enter the annals of history, we do know of other God-dreams from a similar era that confirm the message given to John.

One of the most famous is the dream-vision of a young noblewoman from North Africa named Perpetua. Perpetua was imprisoned for converting to Christianity under a wave of persecution at the turn of the third century and was facing possible execution in the Roman amphitheatre. In her dream, she saw a great bronze ladder reaching high into the heavens. At the base of the ladder lay an enormous snake. With fear and trepidation, Perpetua stood on the head of the snake, and to her surprise it quietly submitted. Then she began to climb the ladder. Each step had to be navigated carefully since the ladder was lined with an arsenal of barbaric weaponry. Finally, she reached the top, where a great crowd cheered her arrival, and a shepherd dressed in white welcomed her with food and drink.[2]

It's not difficult to interpret the meaning of Perpetua's dream. But can you see how it correlates with Revelation? As in John's visions, the dream revealed a spiritual force underlying the brutalities of Roman rule. Rather than a dragon or a beast, the Enemy is depicted as a snake. Like the people of Asia Minor, Perpetua needed to understand the spiritual source of her pain in order to endure it. Like them, she was being called to follow the ways of the Shepherd in spite of the horrors of evil she would face. And just as it was for them, there was the promise of eternal reward.

Today Perpetua's story is told because of the radical grace and kindness she showed her captors. Perpetua's patience and grace in the arena baffled, challenged and drew compassion from the crowd. One of her jailers was even reported to have become a follower of Jesus because of her example.[3] As in the early church, there is victory when we follow the way of the Lamb. The Spirit spoke the same message to more than one.

3. Are Spiritual Signs Following This?

The final test question for discerning the source of our dream-visions asks: 'Are spiritual signs following this?'

How Do You Know It's a God-Dream?

Here we remember that God's words bear the signs of his character. They are filled with divine love and goodness. They carry God's creative power and the ability to bring themselves to pass. Hence, when Holy Spirit speaks in dream-visions, the message will always carry evidence of God's presence.

What sort of 'signs' should we expect? In Peter's vision of the unappetizing lunch, the signs were overtly supernatural. When Peter preached the gospel to the Gentiles at Cornelius's home, they experienced the same miraculous phenomena as the Jews on the Day of Pentecost. The divine message was followed by God's power.

Spiritual signs of God's presence may also be revealed in less 'spectacular' ways. They may include previously unknown information that is later verified or a glimpse of the future that comes to pass. Signs also include elements of wisdom – offering a creative solution or an alternative 'heavenly' way of looking at everyday situations. More broadly, they will exhibit the 'fruit of the Spirit' – such as love, joy, peace, kindness and goodness (Gal. 5:22–23).

In my own journey, I've seen spiritual signs acting as a pointer to the divine source. Sometimes, I would see an unknown scene and it would come to pass the following week. Often, I didn't recognize God's voice until after the events unfolded! This was God's way of teaching me the ways of the Spirit. It also raised my alert levels. While I knew that most dreams weren't the direct voice of God, I was ready to take notice when they were.

Returning to our first-century example: did spiritual signs follow John's visions? Perhaps the simplest way to answer this question is to consider their outcomes. We will explore these in the next chapter. As God's people cooperated with the message of the dream-visions, lives were touched and transformed. The reputation of the church became so distinctive and attractive that it later challenged the forces of the empire itself. Spiritual signs truly followed the word of the Lord.

* * *

How do you know a dream is from God? Ultimately, the message of a true God-dream will always sound like Jesus. God's word hasn't changed since he communicated it through the flesh-life of Jesus two millennia ago. It will always be consistent with his way of self-sacrificial love that overcomes evil. Then, to confirm his word, God will speak his message through others. And when God does, spiritual provision, miracles, healing and the fruit of the Spirit will follow.

After We Wake Up

Listen to the CEO

Diane had been working with a Christian charity for three years when she had an unexpected dream.

In the dream, Diane saw herself in the staff meeting at work. This was a set time of the week when the team gathered for input and encouragement from the organization's leaders. On this day, the meeting was being led by Diane's manager. He read a passage of Scripture, shared a few thoughts, and then asked the staff a question about what it meant to be made in the image of God. Diane felt she knew the answer and eagerly raised her hand. But strangely, the manager dismissed her ideas and belittled her in front of her peers. Diane was shocked and saddened. It seemed as though her opinion didn't matter, and she wondered what she'd done to deserve her boss's rebuke.

But then the CEO of the organization entered the room. He gently nudged Diane's manager to the side and took to the stand. Then he looked directly at Diane, smiled and announced to the group: 'No! Listen to her; *she's right*.'

Then Diane woke up.

The dream lingered with Diane all morning. What did it mean?

Diane didn't need to wait long to find out. At work a few days later, she joined the rest of the staff at their weekly meeting. On this particular day, her manager was leading. He read a passage of Scripture, shared a few thoughts, and then asked the group a question about what it meant to be made in the image of God. Diane raised her hand to answer, but her boss dismissed her ideas and belittled her in front of her peers. She left the staff meeting wondering what she'd done wrong.

Diane's dream had manifested in every way – apart from one key detail.

It was not long after this that Diane was called into her manager's office. She was being dismissed. The news was delivered without reason or explanation. She was to finish at the end of the week.

Diane couldn't understand it. She had worked hard to fulfil her job description and move the organization forward. She had surpassed every key performance indicator and completed new and innovative projects with exceptional feedback. Now she wondered: had she done something wrong?

But look again at the dream! Who was the CEO?

The dream showed that Diane's sudden redundancy was not of her doing. She had got the 'question' right! Her manager may not have seen it, but the One who she was ultimately accountable to – the 'CEO' – had! God was endorsing Diane's motivation and commitment. He had taken her behind the scenes to reassure Diane that she was not the problem.

Soon after she lost her job, Diane remembered a prophecy given to her a few weeks earlier. 'You will be subject to professional jealousy,' the woman had said, 'and you will need to learn to respond with a hard head and a soft heart.'

Diane's experience has all the marks of a God-dream. It passed the foundational test of being consistent with the life and teachings of Jesus – revealing God's perspective and calling Diane to follow the way of the Lamb. The second test question was also answered when the dream's message was confirmed by someone else via prophecy. Finally, the dream was accompanied by spiritual signs in that it provided unknown information about the future that was later verified. The Holy Spirit had spoken to further the ministry of Jesus in Diane's life.

The challenging part of Diane's God-conversation lay in its response. God's call to action was clear but not easy. Diane's experience highlights the fifth and final question of our interpretative framework: *What is the dream asking me to do?*

God-dreams will always require a response. There will be some wisdom to ponder, a change to make or perhaps a new direction to walk in. When God speaks, the goal is always personal transformation and the fulfilment of divine plans. God provides his perspective as we sleep in order to enlist our cooperation when we wake.

In this chapter, we explore the question of our *response* in fulfilling the purpose of our God-dreams. We also look at how this applies to John's visions in Revelation and, finally, what happens when we don't respond at all.

A Crystal Ball or a Relationship?

Diane's dream bore the sovereign hallmark of God's hand because it revealed an aspect of her future. There is nothing quite like seeing a glimpse of what's ahead and then watching it play out before our eyes. This quality of God-speech provokes our curiosity and wonder. Who wouldn't want to know the future? Most of us would love to peer into the crystal ball of the unknown and see who we'll marry, where we'll live or what children we'll bear.

At the same time, this privilege of revelation comes with responsibility. Whether God speaks to reveal a glimpse of the future or whether his message relates to the present and the past, there is a greater purpose beyond just the information. There is always an orientation towards a higher goal. That goal can only be fulfilled when we actively respond.

Perhaps the best way of appreciating the importance of our response to God-speech is to look back on the approach to revelation in the biblical world. Dream-visions and prophetic experiences were not only practised by the people of God. The people of the Ancient Near East and the Greco-Roman world all sought to hear from the gods. It was no strange thing to visit an oracle for a prophecy or seek interpretation for a dream. Hearing from the gods was commonplace. The difference lay in the expected response.

For the world of the Romans, the future was understood to be predetermined and therefore couldn't be changed. Once the oracle had spoken, the omen had been witnessed or the pattern of animal entrails was interpreted, your fate was set. The Hebrew approach was very different. Among God's people, it was understood that God spoke to facilitate *relationship*. This relationship is described in the Old Testament as a 'covenant'. Covenants were made between two parties and functioned as a kind of contract, with each party responsible to the other. In the case of Israel's covenant, God played his part and the Israelites played theirs. Divine conversation came, then, with the understanding that an active response was required. God spoke with intent, and humanity was expected to engage.

When Jesus ushered in the New Covenant, this notion of two-way interaction continued. After Jesus' death, resurrection and ascension, Holy Spirit spoke to call people into relationship – and action. Jesus said we show our love by what we *do* in response to his leading (John 14:21). Indeed, the book of Acts shows how nearly every kingdom activity was preceded by a God-conversation! People heard from God, recognized it as his word and acted on it. It was only then that God's plan manifested in their midst.

In the same way, we are called to respond to God's messages in dream-visions today. Like the apostle Paul, we must not be 'disobedient to the vision from heaven' (Acts 26:19). Ignoring the Holy Spirit has real consequences.

The story of Abraham Lincoln reminds us of how important it is to respond to a God-dream. A few days before his assassination in 1865, Lincoln dreamt of a funeral at the White House. 'Who is dead?' he asked on seeing a body lying in state. 'The President, killed by an assassin!' came the reply.[1]

Sadly, Lincoln lived in a time when God-dreams were not taken seriously. Even though Scripture consistently demonstrates the nature of God's communiqués, Lincoln's western rationalistic paradigm meant that he ignored the dream. Days later, it literally came to pass. Would his death have been averted if he'd responded to the warning? While we don't know for sure, we do know that whenever God speaks, it's with the purpose of enlisting our participation so that his will unfolds in our lives.

Diane tells her own story of heeding the message of her dream. Upon discerning it to be from God, she understood the choice she'd been given: extend forgiveness and grace, or wallow in bitterness and revenge. The call was made all the more difficult when two weeks after her redundancy, a former colleague was promoted to Diane's role, a clear breach of employment law. But in her heart, Diane knew what God was asking. Obeying the Spirit on this occasion meant relinquishing the need to seek the process of law that was rightfully hers. It meant letting go of any need for vindication and moving forward in spite of it.

Diane's decision didn't stop the pain – grace can be a high price to pay. But ultimately her decision resulted in transformation at the deepest level and the establishment of kingdom values in her life. For Diane, a 'hard head' meant facing the truth and not denying the wrong done against her, and a 'soft heart' meant showing humility and love to her former employer anyway. While it wasn't easy, Diane would say it was well worth the cost. This experience and others like it have shaped her character and set her free from the prison of offence. It isn't surprising that years later, God has vindicated her choices and promoted her into higher levels of leadership and influence. Blessing comes when we hear God's voice and follow (John 10:27).

05) What Was the Dream Asking John and the Asian Churches to Do?

The importance of the fifth question in the God Dreams framework is also seen in the response of the Asian churches to John's dream-visions. His revelations contained profound spiritual truths, but they also called for an active response. So, what specifically was God asking John and the Asian churches to do?

We've seen that Holy Spirit was calling the Christians of Asia Minor to align themselves to the way of the Lamb rather than the idolatrous beast. This meant pledging loyalty to the One who sat on the throne of heaven rather than the one who sat on the throne of Rome. In exalting God's king of kings over the world's 'king of kings', the church would live a different way.

In practice, for early Christians this meant allowing the self-sacrificial love of the Lamb to shape every aspect of their lives. It meant clothing themselves in the 'robes' of righteous acts and fighting evil with the words of God's truth. As they did, they would become participants in God's army and share in Jesus' victory over an empire that seemed as invincible as a seven-headed dragon. Their actions would destroy the forces of evil that drove the injustice and oppression around them and bring God's kingdom from heaven to earth. Evil and suffering would be defied as they acted in love and grace.

They might not always see the victory of their efforts at first, as evil rallied to survive, but in time, justice would be served and they would experience the fullness of an unhindered relationship with God. Their reward would be a celebration as rapturous as a wedding feast, a home as stunning as a bejewelled city, and provision as bountiful as a garden that never fails to produce.

John's dream-visions invited the church to uncompromising faithfulness. It was not an easy call. It might even cost their lives. To reject the gods of empire was to strike at the heart of Rome, inviting rejection from family and friends and the condemnation of civil leaders. Following the Lamb's ways of love and forgiveness would appear weak and pathetic against the Enemy's ferocity and might. But then they would see God's true reality. They would experience the strength of the lamb with seven horns and the wisdom of a lamb with seven eyes. Evil would be overcome as the heavenly kingdom manifested all around them. The result would be transformation that would extend far beyond their own natural lives and communities.

The question is: did they do it?

History tells us of their breathtaking response. Today we read the stories of the early church in the annals of history. We see that as time passed, the church became known for its good deeds. The early Christians reached out generously to the weak, caring for the widows and orphans, and clothing the poor. In times of plague and disease, they tended the sick and gathered the abandoned. In a world where weakness was mocked and the poor were discarded, the church's actions were unique and confronting. This was the bride, not the prostitute; the lamb, not the beast.

And so the church grew in influence and stature. Soon it became clear that the ways of God's kingdom conflicted with the ways of selfish humanity, and the empire began to fight back. During the second and third centuries, Roman persecution periodically engulfed the church with brutal consequences. Yet through it all, the followers of Jesus refused to buckle under the lure of the beast. As John's dream-visions had exhorted them to do, they denied allegiance to the emperor, preferring to be marked only by 'the seal of God'. Martyrdom was not uncommon under the mercilessness of the Roman sword.

But the story did not end there. Historians tell us that the actions of the early church set into motion the shaping of western values for centuries to come. This was the beginning of the ideals we prize so highly today. Compassion for neighbours, the sanctity of life and the principle of equal justice are all based on the self-sacrificing actions and teachings of the Lamb.[2] The kingdom of God had truly begun to come from heaven to earth as the Spirit had promised.

Of course, the scenes described in the final chapters of John's God-conversations have yet to be fully realized. The visions of Revelation continue to call God's people to active response today. The human kingdoms of this world still thrive on greed, selfishness and injustice. Abuse of power and love of wealth drive the systems of contemporary governments and societies. As in the early church, the weapons of God's kingdom continue to be offered to us. Every time we act in accordance with the Lamb's ways, we engage in spiritual battle. When we love in the face of hatred, forgive in times of offence, and reach out in generosity to the sick, the poor and the rejected, we take ground from the Enemy and usher in God's kingdom. Like the people of Asia Minor, we become one of the partying crowd, taking our place in God's army and, one day, sharing in the fruit of God's reward and justice. The call to respond to John's revelation lives on.

When We Don't Respond

One question remains: what happens when we don't respond?

Whenever God speaks, grace is always present. The beauty of God's nature is that Holy Spirit forever offers an open invitation. While God never changes the call, there is patience and grace even in our resistance. Unconditional love drives God to persevere as long as there is hope. All the while, the call to follow Jesus' continuing voice remains.

In the case of our natural dreams, the call to respond is also present. Many times, a dream recurs in different ways until we take notice. The alert continues to flash, reminding us of any unresolved issues and pointing us towards wholeness. We saw this in the testimony of the elderly woman who dreamed of waiting for her husband to take the wheel of her car (Chapter 8). This dream repeated itself for several years after her husband's death before she finally responded. Similarly, those who have experienced trauma or life-changing events in their past may often experience recurring dreams that call them to respond.

The power of dream-visions lies in what we do with them. Once they've been interpreted and discerned, the onus is on us to act. If they are from God, will we cooperate and submit to his call on our lives? If they are from ourselves (and carry a coherent message), will we work with them towards healing and wholeness? If they arise from ungodly spirits, will we look at why they have come, repent, and resist them?

God-dreams in particular show us a way to live that radically blesses our lives and the lives of others. But the impact of dream-visions will always be dependent on what we do with them. The onus is on us to see visionary experiences as a potential vehicle of growth and impact, particularly when they are sourced in God. As the angel said to John in the final scenes of his life-changing revelations: '*Blessed is the one* who keeps the words of the prophecy written in this scroll' (Rev. 22:7, italics mine).

Meeting God in a Dream

A Terrorist Meets Jesus

Ahmed[1] was an ISIS terrorist who revelled in killing Christians.[2] Along with fellow members of the ISIS organization, he was responsible for an endless string of gory deeds involving beheadings, hangings and stonings, with the goal of establishing an Islamic state across the Middle East.

But then Ahmed began having dreams of a man in white. In the dreams, the man spoke to him: 'You are killing my people.'

Afterwards, Ahmed began feeling uneasy about his actions, and his convictions began to weaken. Even so, he continued his murderous pursuit. On one occasion, a victim insisted on giving Ahmed his Bible before dying at his hand. Still more dreams of the man in white followed. Ahmed began reading his Bible. In time, he decided to follow Christ.

Similar stories to Ahmed's have emerged from the Middle East. One of my favourites concerns a young woman named Aisha.[3] Aisha was on her *haj* to Mecca, the once-in-a-lifetime pilgrimage that all faithful Muslims aspire to complete as part of their commitment to Islam. While dozing off in her tent one night, Aisha had a vision. A man dressed in white entered her tent and stood before her. At first, she thought it was a visiting cleric, but then she realized there was no opening in her tent. In his presence, she experienced a deep and tangible sense of love. Somehow Aisha knew the man was Jesus. In time, more dreams of Jesus came, each beckoning her to follow.

Missiologists suggest that between 30% and 50% of Muslims in the Middle East who have made a decision to follow Jesus have done so because of a God-dream.[4] Many of the dream-visions share common features: Jesus appears; he is dressed in white; the dreamers feel a deep sense of love. Typically, the dream marks a turning point in their spiritual journey, culminating in the recognition that this man is more than just the prophet they've heard about in Islam. Thousands have surrendered their lives to Jesus as a result.

In this chapter we explore the idea that God speaks in dream-visions to those who don't know him. It appears that God takes the sovereign initiative to bring his message of good news to the world. People can meet Jesus in a dream!

But this doesn't mean we have no role to play. When we learn to recognize God's voice in our own dream-visions, we can help others do the same. We can also hear from God in dream-visions on behalf of other people. When we do, we will see God's kingdom come to earth in their lives as well as ours.

Jesus on the Crystal Floor

In the early years of God Conversations, I was inspired by the testimonies of people like Ahmed and Aisha. I wondered if God could be speaking in the same way in my part of the world. It made sense that if God was speaking to those who didn't know him in the Middle East, he might be speaking to those who didn't know him in Australia. So I decided to check it out.

The opportunity came when I was invited to minister in a church in Queensland, one of the northern states of Australia. The church was located in the centre of a beautiful coastal town that attracted the spiritual and the searching. Many of them practised New Age forms of spirituality and were open to the spiritual realm. The church had a deep heart for their community so when I mentioned the God Dreams community seminar, they jumped right in. Here was the moment I was waiting for.

First, we trained the church to recognize God's voice in their own dream-visions. Then we hosted an event for the community at a building in the centre of town. It was a relatively small gathering of about fifteen attendees. Among them were tarot card readers, psychics and spiritual healers.

My approach was to teach the group how to interpret the language of their dreams and use dreams as a pathway towards wholeness. We talked about the ABCs of symbols and the five questions of the God Dreams framework, using many of my own God-dreams as examples.

Towards the end of the seminar, I suggested that there is a God who wants to speak to us, and one of his favoured modes of communication is dream-visions. Many were surprised to hear of a God who speaks so personally. Perhaps God was speaking to them in their dreams!

After the first session, one of the group came up to chat: 'Could you help me understand my dream?' The dream had come twice that month and impacted her deeply upon waking. In the dream, she saw a room in her home with a beautiful crystal floor. In the centre of the room stood a man dressed in white. He had dark wavy hair and gleaming eyes. 'I've never felt the presence of such pure love as I have in that dream,' she said. 'Perhaps you can tell me who the man is?'

I shouldn't have been surprised. The God who was speaking to Muslims in the Middle East was speaking to New Age practitioners in Australia. This is a God who is forever reaching out.

God's Dream Outreach

The fact that God speaks to those outside the church may come as a surprise to us, but it shouldn't. In biblical history, God spoke frequently to those who didn't know him!

Consider how God spoke in a dream to *King Abimelech*, warning him not to take Sarah as his wife because she was already married to Abram (Gen. 20:1–7), and later, how God spoke in a dream about the heavenly stairway to *Jacob* who was alienated from God (Gen. 28:10–22). Moving on to the time of Joseph, recall how God spoke to the *Egyptian pharaoh* about the coming drought using the imagery of fat and skinny cows (Gen. 41:1–7), and then, in the period of the judges, God spoke in a dream to two *Midianite soldiers* to affirm Gideon's victory (Judg. 7:13–14)! Then later, during the Babylonian exile, think of how God spoke in a dream to *King Nebuchadnezzar* about his obnoxious pride (Dan. 4), as well as his son, *Belshazzar*, through a vision of handwriting on the wall (Dan. 5). Moving into the time of Jesus, recall how God spoke in a dream to the *wise men* from the east with a warning about King Herod's murderous plot (Matt. 2:12), and later to *Pilate's wife* to alert her about the innocence of Jesus (Matt. 27:19).

In many of these cases, God spoke to those who didn't know him in order to protect his covenant people and the promises he had made to them. It is when Jesus comes to usher in the New Covenant that we begin to see more clearly God's motivation for speaking to those who don't know him. As the living 'Word of God' in the flesh, Jesus was constantly on the lookout for those who were seeking revelation and understanding. God's heart for outsiders was on display in Jesus' conversation with the Samaritan woman at the well (John 4:1–26), the healing of the Syrophoenician woman (Mark 7:24–29) and Jesus' interaction with a Roman centurion (Matt. 8:5–13). The God revealed in Jesus is an outreaching God who left his dwelling place in heaven to be birthed into a Jewish home so that he could engage personally with humanity.

God's heart to reach people outside the Jewish nation continued beyond Jesus' death, resurrection and ascension. After the Holy Spirit was poured out on the church on the Day of Pentecost, we see one of the most dramatic incidences of God speaking to those who don't know him with Paul's radical conversion on the Damascus Road. Like Ahmed of today, Paul the apostle was once Saul the terrorist, but was stopped in his tracks by a visionary experience (Acts 9:1–18; 26:19).

Finally, we see God speaking to *Cornelius* in a vision. Like Paul, Cornelius was not a believer in Jesus, but a 'God-fearer' who longed to know God personally. Cornelius' vision of an angel led to a meeting with the apostle Peter, an introduction to the gospel and, finally, a decision to follow Jesus (Acts 10).

These testimonies of Spirit-inspired dream-visions are radical demonstrations of God's heart for all humanity. Since the Holy Spirit speaks as the continuing voice of Jesus, it shouldn't be surprising that God speaks to those who don't know him. The Spirit continues what Jesus has always done (John 14:26). The God of the Bible hasn't changed. God longs to reveal himself to those who don't know him and, it seems, he freely uses dream-visions to do it!

Helping Others to See

Since that first God Dreams seminar in Queensland, I have conducted many more dream events for the community in partnership with local churches, as well as private gatherings and 'Mind, Body, Spirit' festivals in my capital city. Each time, I am struck by the interest in spirituality and the desire for something more. At the festivals, the queues for psychic readings wind all the way back to the entrance, and the halls are packed with everything in the spiritual supermarket, from angel aura paintings to computerized palm readings and Egyptian raindrop cleansing. Each time I have taught in places like these, people have realized that dreams may offer us more than a hangover from a spicy meal, and are drawn to hear God's voice as they sleep.

God may be speaking to people in your community, too. Like Jacob fleeing his brother in the desert, Paul travelling the Damascus Road and Ahmed on his terrorist pursuit, the Spirit is reaching out to draw people closer to himself. God's heart is to bring the good news of Jesus into all the world. So, what part do we have to play?

We begin by acknowledging that the Holy Spirit is already at work, revealing himself to those in our communities who don't know him personally. God could be introducing himself to your family and friends in dreams! Like Joseph, Daniel and Peter of old, we can participate in the process by helping others to recognize the Spirit as they sleep.

Here, it is important to remember that the language of dreams operates the *same way* in everyone, irrespective of their faith journey. That is, the nature of symbolism isn't dependent on the source of our dreams. There is not a special sanctified form of language for God-dreams and a different one for natural dreams. Hence, once we have learned to understand and interpret our own dreams, we are well equipped to help others.

When someone shares their dream with us, we can use the God Dreams framework to reflect on it together. The key is to work with the dreamer to lead them to their *own* interpretation. One of our biggest errors is to impose our own ideas on a dream-vision without the dreamer's consultation (unless it comes as a *separate revelation* of the Holy Spirit).[5]

This involves asking plenty of questions and allowing even more time to listen. We should ask the dreamer about the setting of the dream ('What is going on in your life right now?'), and the feelings in the dream and any changes in them ('How did you feel in the dream?'). Then we work with the symbols by helping the dreamer identify the key images and their relevance to the dreamer ('What do the symbols mean to you?'). Here we are seeking an 'aha' moment – remembering that the interpretation always belongs to the dreamer.

By then, we can consider the origin of the dream, asking: 'Where do you think the dream came from?' The answer will help determine the response. Asking the question may also provide an opportunity to share God's heart with the person.

Finally, there will be a call to respond. Even the messages of natural dreams invite us to enlist God's help. There may be fears to address, resolutions to be strengthened and emotional issues to be worked through. An offer to pray might be appropriate.

At one of our God Dreams events, a woman shared a recurring dream she had experienced since the time of her childhood. Details differed each time, but the theme was always the same. In the dreams, she would see herself driving a car along a winding road. Her younger brother was riding alongside her. After a time, she would veer towards a cliff. Just as the car was about to tip over the edge, she would wake up in terror.

After sharing her dream with me, we talked through the different elements of the dream. Upon hearing her backstory, the meaning became clear. The woman had lost both her parents as a child, and the fear of losing her brother haunted her. The dream came to alert her to the unresolved concerns of her heart. Although it was not a God-dream per se, the woman had a semblance of faith and allowed me to pray for God's help in quelling the fear she had carried all her life.

These kinds of experiences may also point to issues that would benefit from the guidance of a professional counsellor. You never know what might come up in dreams! The key is to be open to the possibility that God might be speaking to those around us in dream-visions and be ready to help point them in the right direction.

A Gift of Interpretation?

Some people speak of a 'spiritual gift' of dream interpretation. The idea comes from the lives of Joseph and Daniel in the Old Testament. Both their stories highlight the ability to interpret dreams as coming from God (Gen. 41:16–39; Dan. 1:17; 2:28; 4:18). So, is there a special gift of interpretation?

There is no specific mention of a gift of dream interpretation in the 'gift lists' of the New Testament writings. However, we do know that God has appointed prophets in the church to lead in this area and, specifically, to train others to hear God's voice and prophesy (Eph. 4:12). Prophets are *specialists* who are called to help others embrace the fullness of the revelatory Spirit. For some prophets, and in my own experience, the ability to interpret a message in symbolic language comes easily. Our job is to help others hear God's voice for themselves.

In acknowledging the gifting of prophets, we must always remember that God has given *everyone* who follows Jesus the ability to hear God's voice in dream-visions (Acts 2:16–17). We must not revert to the ways of the Old Covenant in thinking that a specialist is always required to interpret our experiences. The specialist anointing of the prophets is primarily to equip others. As we have seen, interpretation is a skill that can be *learned*.

Dreaming for Others

We have explored how God may speak directly in dream-visions to those who don't know him, but God may also use *our* dream-visions to speak to others.

In a dream, Michelle saw herself walking in a park when she met an old friend. Her friend was sitting on a bench sobbing uncontrollably. Beside her friend was a creepy hobbit-like man crouching on his haunches. He had his arm tightly around her.

Michelle asked her friend if she was okay, but the hobbit-like man answered in a menacing, hissing voice and pushed her away. In response, Michelle spoke boldly and without fear: 'No! You go away! She's *my* friend.'

The next day, Michelle phoned her friend and left a message, telling her about the dream and saying she was praying for her. Her friend didn't call back, so Michelle thought nothing more of it.

Two weeks later, Michelle's friend returned the call. She hadn't responded to Michelle's message because the dream had shocked and unnerved her. The friend went on to explain that she had been experiencing deep depression – the worse she had ever had – but on the day of Michelle's call, the sadness had suddenly lifted.

At the time, Michelle was unaware of her friend's mental struggles. She didn't even know God spoke in dream-visions! Michelle's story shows how God can speak to others through our dream-visions. In this way, our visionary experiences become *prophecy*

(Acts 2:17; 1 Cor. 14). God calls us to deliver the message and, in so doing, minister to and encourage another person.

The beauty of this process is its orientation towards *others*. The apostle Paul wrote that the prophetic gifting is the most desirable of all gifts because it strengthens, encourages and comforts people around us (1 Cor. 14:3). When a revelatory message is delivered in love and is consistent with the living Word Jesus, it has great power to build up others' lives.

A word of caution here, however. Whenever we receive a visionary message involving another person, it is important to first pray and consider if the message is *for us*. As we have seen, people in our dream-visions can act as a symbol, reflecting a part of ourselves. Most dreams that feature other people are about us!

Before we act on the dream of another person, ask: 'Is this dream about me?' Only after confirming that it's not, should we act on it. On some occasions, prayer may be the most appropriate response. Whenever there's a leading to share the dream, it should only be done in a spirit of humility and submission. Ultimately, interpretation and discernment always belongs to the person receiving the revelation.

* * *

When we remember that the Holy Spirit speaks in dream-visions as Jesus' continuing voice, we will understand that God is constantly reaching out to others with his message of life and truth. Learning how to understand our own dream-visions will equip us to help others in their journey. As in the Middle East, may we see many of those around us meeting God in a dream!

Awakening Your Dreams

Early in my ministry, I would regularly ask the congregations I visited if they found it difficult to hear from God. At least 80% of them would raise their hands. The frustration and angst on their faces was clear. It's not uncommon for people to struggle to recognize the voice of the Spirit.

Perhaps God-dreams are part of the solution. After all, all we need to do is switch off the light, lay our heads on the pillow and close our eyes. *Zzzz*. Next morning as the light begins to filter through the window, a voice may be heard.

As we have seen, *everybody dreams*, whether we recognize it or not. Hearing God in dreams makes his voice accessible to anyone – we all have to sleep sometime!

In this final chapter, we look at how to hear from God more clearly and regularly in dream-visions. As the author of Job wrote, God *is* speaking in this way – the problem is we don't *recognize* it (Job 33:13-15). It's as though we are *asleep* to God's voice. But with the right understanding, we can 'awaken our dreams' – we can wake up to the reality of God's voice as we sleep.

To hear God's voice more clearly in dream-visions, we need to revisit the key to hearing God's voice in general. For this, we turn to a scene in the life of Jesus.

A Preaching Blooper

News had spread quickly. The great Rabbi Jesus was nearby! Locals were keen to hear his message and gathered in small groups by the lake. The sound of animated conversation rose as more and more joined the throng.

Suddenly, the crowd's attention was drawn to a disturbance by the water. A fishing boat had been set loose and was moving along the shore closer to the group. Inside the boat stood a man, his face poised and robes swaying in the breeze.

It's Jesus!

The rabbi checked his balance and began to speak. He spoke of familiar scenes. A sower scattering seed in preparation for harvest. Some seed was welcomed by rich and moist soil. Other seed was rejected by thorny roots and dry ground.

The story was coming to a close. The crowd leaned in, eyes and ears peeled.

Jesus paused. He peered out across the mass of earnest faces and declared in a loud voice, 'Whoever has ears, let them hear!'

Then he sat down.

Jesus' disciples took up the oars and rowed the boat away from the shore.

A frustrated murmur reverberated through the crowd.

'What?' said one. 'I don't get it!'

'What was his point?' said another, shrugging his shoulders in dismay.

With confusion on their faces, the crowd began to disperse, brushing the dust off their robes and walking away (Mark 4:1–20; Matt. 13:1–23).

* * *

In my years of working in Bible colleges, we trained thousands of students in the art of preaching. The subject was known as 'Homiletics' and involved teaching them how to expound Scripture and share the gospel. In our classes, we would encourage the students to speak clearly and simply. The main goal was to get the message across. A fail in Homiletics was to leave the audience scratching their heads and screwing up their faces in confusion.

Like Jesus did.

It's a befuddling scene. Why would Jesus go to all the effort of securing the attention of the crowd, eloquently tell a story, and then neglect to mention the key point?

Jesus often did this. He taught in parables and used metaphorical language where the meaning wasn't immediately obvious.

The question is: why? Why shroud such an important message in mystery? Why leave the crowd hanging?

Ears to Hear and Eyes to See

The story of Jesus' sermon by the lake and others like it tell us that Jesus knew something we often don't. The answer lies in his final statement: 'Whoever has ears, let them hear.' This phrase is used on twelve occasions in the Gospels and eight times in the book of Revelation! It is the key to hearing God's voice more clearly.

In these words, Jesus directs us to the pathway of spiritual hearing and seeing. Revelation doesn't come from storing up vaults of theoretical knowledge, obeying the rules or belonging to the right crowd. Revelation comes through *seeking*. It flows out of the position of our hearts. It reflects a decision we make to listen, watch and heed God's voice.

There were two groups who heard Jesus' message about the sower and the seed that day. The first group walked away in ignorance, dismissing the message because it didn't make sense. The second group sought to know the truth of Jesus' words. They went back and asked Jesus what he meant (see Mark 4:10): 'Jesus, what did you mean when you talked about the different types of soil? What is the significance of the seeds that took root and the seeds that died?' And because they were hungry to know, they received the answers.

The behaviour of the second group provides us with an example to follow. Whether it be through dream-visions, an internal voice or some other mode of communication, the key to hearing the Spirit lies in the positioning of our hearts. Those who have ears to hear will hear. Those who have eyes to see will see. It is a matter of attentiveness accompanied by the desire to follow. Jesus said that his people recognize his voice *and* they follow (John 10:27, italics mine).

This approach calls us to frame hearing God's voice in the context of *relationship*. When we understand that God's overriding purpose in speaking is to develop relationship, we won't be tempted to seek a God-dream for the sake of a supernatural experience. Our motivation won't be to discover unknown knowledge, have power over another, see into the future or even prove God's existence. If we follow that path, we become like those in the ancient world who used dreams to manipulate the future or control their circumstances.[1]

Of course, God-dreams *are* supernatural. There is nothing quite like witnessing the in-breaking of God's power and wisdom in our natural situations. But the goal never lies with the experience itself. The goal is encountering the One who sent it. As a God defined by love (1 John 4:8), God's act of speaking always serves the purpose of relationship. Knowing this, our posture will be shaped by the same goal. We will be willing to listen to God whatever the message. The position of our heart enables us to hear.

Hearing the Spirit begins with a singular desire to know God and hear his voice. As in the writings of old, the call remains: 'which of them has stood in the council of the LORD to see or to hear his word?' (Jer. 23:18). In other words, who will have their ears peeled, listening for God's voice, as they go to sleep, drive to work, wash the dishes – as they go about the everyday happenings of their lives? Who among us has eyes to see and ears to hear?

How to Awaken Your Dreams

After positioning our hearts, we need to be *open* to hearing God's voice in dream-visions. Part of this is simply awareness. Once we realize that God speaks in visual ways, we will be more likely to notice it. The poetry of the Song of Songs describes it well: 'I slept but my heart was awake' (Song 5:2). We need to be *awake* to the possibility that God could be calling for us in the night.

Having established our motivation for seeking a God-dream, there are some practical steps to take. The first is simply to join the conversation. In faith, we need to ask God to speak to us. Having faith means believing the promise that the Spirit was given to everyone: sons and daughters, young and old (Acts 2:17). This may involve asking God a specific question before we turn the lights out. 'Lord, please speak to me tonight about . . .' Asking a question tunes our heart for an answer.

Second, we need to take notice of our dreams when we wake. Most dreams are forgotten within the first ten to fifteen minutes of getting out of bed. By the time we take our shower and make the coffee, they're likely to have disappeared. So it's helpful to get into the habit of checking our dreams as we wake up. God will often speak to us in those half-waking moments. This may also involve switching off our alarm clocks now and then, as alarms tend to interrupt the last dream we have – and the one we're most likely to remember.

Third, we need to write down significant dreams. The book of Habakkuk tells us to: 'Write down the vision; make it plain so you can run with it' (see Hab. 2:2). Writing down our dream-visions allows us to reflect on them in the days to come. Details in the dream often come to life and make more sense with the passage of time. As we reflect on them, we may be able to identify patterns, recurring themes or repetitive symbols that we might have missed had we not recorded them. Of course, this does not mean journalling every dream we have! Not every dream is of equal value. It's best to focus on the dreams that have some sort of emotional impact and where the message seems to linger. As time goes on, we will get more proficient at recognizing our most significant dreams.

Fourth, we need to meditate on the meaning. Use the God Dreams framework of five questions to reflect on the setting, feeling, symbols, source and response in the dream. This process involves time, prayer and reflection with trusted friends and confidantes. Revelation often comes as we talk through the details of an experience with another person.

The final step is to apply the message. There is very little value in discerning and interpreting our dream-visions if we miss the final act. God's power, love and creativity is released when we cooperate in faith with his messages.

THE GOD-DREAMS FRAMEWORK

01 Setting
What is happening in my life?

02 Emotions
How did I feel in the dream?

03 Symbols
What do the symbols mean to me?

04 Source
Where did the dream come from?

05 Response
What is the dream asking me to do?

What Do You See?

Early in the life of the prophet Jeremiah, God asked him a question: 'What do you see?' (Jer. 1:11). The answer revealed a life-changing perspective on what God was doing in the story of Israel and went on to direct Jeremiah's role in it.

Perhaps the most important factor in awakening our dreams is to answer that question for ourselves. *What do I see?* Through the Holy Spirit, God gives us the ability to see with heavenly eyes.

Several years ago, I had a dream that taught me the difference it makes when we see from God's perspective. In the dream, I saw myself singing in church when suddenly the building began to collapse all around me. People screamed as the walls crumbled and dust filled the air. In a panic, I began to run, joining the terrified crowd in a race to the exit. It was a relief to make it onto the street.

But my relief was short-lived. I had hardly taken a breath before noticing a series of bombs flying through the air. The city was under attack! Again, I took off, sprinting through the streets in fear for my life, ever conscious of the sound of missiles whistling in my ears.

Then the scene changed. I saw myself sheltering behind a large rock, far from the city. From here, I could look back in safety and watch the flaming tails of the missiles darting in and around the buildings. I braced for the inevitable explosions, thankful that I had escaped.

But as I continued to watch the scene, I noticed something strange. The bombs weren't detonating. They continued to threaten, but they didn't blow up. *What was going on? Maybe it was safe to stay in the city after all?*

Then I woke up.

At the time of my dream, several events had threatened to derail God's plans for my life. It looked like everything was 'blowing up in my face'. But through the vision, God gave me insight into his perspective. Underlying the natural events of my situation was a spiritual battle. Menacing as it appeared, God was saying it wouldn't have any impact on my future. Missiles might threaten but they weren't going to blow! So I was to stand firm and not leave my post.

The dream completely changed my view of the events around me. It lifted me up from my circumstances and allowed me to live beyond the difficulty and pain of the season.

The beauty of God's New Covenant is that God has given us eyes to see what he is doing. He speaks to us so that we may know how to respond in line with his plan. God comes to each one of us and asks: *What do you see?*

The question is reminiscent of John's vision in the throne room with the four winged creatures. The creatures were 'covered with eyes' – all over the front of their bodies, over their backs, and even under their wings! (Rev. 4:6–8). These creatures had eyes to see. They saw the reality of the world around them with truth and clarity.

Awakening Your Dreams

Like the winged creatures in God's throne room, we have been invited to see with God's eyes. The Holy Spirit gives us the ability to see beyond the natural and physical realm. We can enter the council of God and know what he is doing. The revelation then equips us to live a different way.

This is the beauty of the New Covenant – the inheritance God has for each one of us. Let's not miss the vision God wants to reveal. The Holy Spirit is speaking in creative, symbolic and masterful ways to continue the ministry and mission of Jesus. Let us be people who are 'covered with eyes'! Looking, waiting, seeking, listening and watching. God's question to the prophet Jeremiah yet remains: 'What do you see?'

Notes

1. The First Time I Had a God-Dream

[1] John Loren Sandford, *Elijah Among Us: Understanding and Responding to God's Prophets Today* (Grand Rapids, MI: Chosen, 2002), p. 163.

[2] Wilda B. Tanner, *The Mystical, Magical, Marvelous World of Dreams* (Tahlequah, OK: Sparrow Hawk Press, 1988), p. 10.

[3] For a review of the topic of dreams and visions in Pentecostal-Charismatic academic literature showing its neglect, see Tania M. Harris, *Hearing God's Voice: Towards a Theology of Contemporary Pentecostal Revelatory Experience* (Leiden: Brill, 2023), p. 23.

[4] For more on this prophetic process in biblical history, see Tania Harris, *The Church who Hears God's Voice: Equipping Everyone to Recognise and Respond to the Spirit* (Milton Keynes: Paternoster, 2022), pp. 7–8.

2. What Are Dreams and Visions?

[1] In 1953, an article was published in *Science* that reported the laboratory findings of Nathaniel Kleitman, who used the encephalograph to monitor dreaming. This publication gave new impetus to dream research. Sleep and dream laboratories began to spring up, and within twenty years, more than twenty-five of them were operating in the USA alone: Louis M. Savary, Patricia H. Berne and Strephon Kaplan Williams, *Dreams and Spiritual Growth: A Judeo-Christian Way of Dreamwork* (New York, NY: Paulist Press), p. 66. Also see Google Books N-gram Viewer for interest among the general

Notes

population: https://books.google.com/ngrams/graph?content=dreams&year_start=1800&year_end=2019&corpus=en-2019&smoothing=3 (accessed 15 Jan. 2024).

2. Morton T. Kelsey, *God, Dreams, and Revelation: A Christian Interpretation of Dreams* (Minneapolis, MN: Augsburg Fortress, 1991), p. 187.

3. Recent studies point to the reasons why some remember their dreams and others may not: Sander van der Linden, 'The Science behind Dreaming', *Scientific American* (26 July 2011) https://www.scientificamerican.com/article/the-science-behind-dreaming (accessed 8 Nov. 2023).

4. There is significant evidence that animals dream, although of course we cannot be certain: Cody Cottier, 'Do Animals Dream and How Can We Tell?' *Discover* (9 Sept. 2023) https://www.discovermagazine.com/planet-earth/do-animals-dream-and-how-can-we-tell (accessed 8 Sept. 2023).

5. Kelsey, *God, Dreams, and Revelation*, pp. 187–8.

6. Osman Shabir, 'Why Do We Dream?' *News Medical* (2021) www.news-medical.net/health/Why-Do-We-Dream.aspx (accessed 16 Nov. 2021).

7. Shabir, 'Why Do We Dream?'

8. Tore Nielsen and Russell A. Powell, 'Dreams of the Rarebit Fiend: Food and Diet as Instigators of Bizarre and Disturbing Dreams', *Frontiers in Psychology* 6 (2015) https://www.academia.edu/10605094/Dreams_of_the_Rarebit_Fiend_food_and_diet_as_instigators_of_bizarre_and_disturbing_dreams_2015_ (accessed 14 March 2024).

9. Kelsey, *God, Dreams, and Revelation*, p. 188. Also Shabir, 'Why Do We Dream?'

10. Quoted in John A. Sanford, *Dreams: God's Forgotten Language* (New York, NY: HarperCollins, rev. edn, 1989), p. 98.

11. Sandee LaMotte, 'Our Dreams Are Changing as We Emerge from the Pandemic. Here's How', *CNN* (14 July 2023) https://edition.cnn.com/2021/07/12/health/dreams-pandemic-opening-wellness/index.html (accessed 14 Sept. 2021).

12. Hospice & Palliative Care, Buffalo, 'Study Conducted by The Palliative Care Institute Indicates Dreams and Visions Provide a Profound Source of Meaning and Comfort for the Dying' (3 Apr. 2022) https://www.hospicebuffalo.com/news/press-releases/study-conducted-palliative-care-institute-indicates-dreams-and-visions-provide-profound-source-meaning-and-comfort-dying (accessed 14 Mar. 2024).

13. Carl Jung, *The Psychology of the Unconscious* (1916), now published as C.G. Jung, *Collected Works, vol. 5: Symbols of Transformation* (New York, NY: Random House/Pantheon, 1956).

[14] Kelsey, *God, Dreams, and Revelation*, p. 171, referencing Sigmund Freud, *The Interpretation of Dreams* (New York, NY: Basic, 1995) and *A General Introduction to Psychoanalysis* (New York, NY: Washington Square Press, 1960).

[15] Kelsey, *God, Dreams, and Revelation*, p. 20.

[16] Montague Ullman and Stanley Krippner, *Dream Telepathy* (New York, NY: Macmillan, 1973), referenced in Louis M. Savary, Patricia H. Berne and Strephon Kaplan Williams, *Dreams and Spiritual Growth: A Judeo-Christian Way of Dreamwork* (New York, NY: Paulist Press, 1984), p. 209.

[17] Kelsey, *God, Dreams, and Revelation*, p. 55, referencing the work of Mircea Eliade, *Myths, Dreams and Mysteries* (New York, NY: Harper & Brothers, 1960).

[18] Jean-Marie Husser, *Dreams and Dream Narratives in the Biblical World* (Sheffield: Sheffield Academic Press, 2001), p. 18.

[19] Kelly Bulkeley, *Dreaming in the World's Religions: A Comparative History* (New York, NY: New York University Press, 2008).

[20] 'Dreams and visions' were the 'accredited media of prophetic revelation' from the time of Moses: Roger Stronstad, *The Prophethood of All Believers: A Study in Luke's Charismatic Theology*, Journal of Pentecostal Theology Supplement 16 (Sheffield: Sheffield Academic Press, 1999), p. 69; Max Turner, *The Holy Spirit and Spiritual Gifts: In the New Testament Church and Today* (Grand Rapids, MI: Baker Academic, rev. edn, 2012), pp. 8, 194.

[21] Sandford, *Elijah Among Us*, p. 163.

[22] John B.F. Miller, *Convinced That God Had Called Us: Dreams, Visions and the Perception of God's Will in Luke-Acts* (Leiden/Boston: Brill, 2007), pp. 11–13.

[23] Kelsey, *God, Dreams and Revelation*, pp. 32–4, 87.

[24] *Hozeh* meaning 'seer' is the oldest term. The term *nabi* is more common: David E. Aune, *Prophecy in Early Christianity and the Ancient Mediterranean World* (Grand Rapids, MI: Eerdmans, 1983), p. 83. In 1 Chr. 29:29, both terms are used: 'seer' and 'prophet'.

[25] Earlier in biblical history, a form of divination using the Urim and Thummin (sacred stones kept on the high priest's breastplate) was also an option, but this method of guidance is extremely rare in the Old Testament (1 Sam. 28:6).

[26] Miller, *Convinced That God Had Called Us*, pp. 167–233.

[27] Kelsey, *God, Dreams, and Revelation*, p. 90.

[28] Johannes Lindblom, *Prophecy in Ancient Israel* (Philadelphia, PA: Fortress, 1962), p. 108; Miller, *Convinced That God Had Called Us*, pp. 11–13; Kelsey, *God, Dreams, and Revelation*, p. 33; Ben Witherington III, *Jesus the Seer: The Progress of Prophecy* (Peabody, MA: Hendrickson, 1999), p. 7; Shaul Bar, *A Letter That Has Not Been Read: Dreams in the Hebrew Bible* (Cincinnati, OH: Hebrew Union College Press, 2001), p. 143.

[29] Lindblom, *Prophecy in Ancient Israel*, p. 108.
[30] Kelsey, *God, Dreams, and Revelation*, pp. 32–4, 87.

3. The Language of Dream-Visions

[1] Rachel Gillett, 'Why We're More Likely to Remember Content with Images and Video', *Fast Company* (18 Sept. 2014) https://www.fastcompany.com/3035856/why-were-more-likely-to-remember-content-with-images-and-video-infogr (accessed 12 Nov. 2020).
[2] Barbara Cerf-Ducastel and Claire Murphy, 'Neural Substrates of Cross-modal Olfactory Recognition Memory: An fMRI Study', *Neuroimage* 31.1 (2006), pp. 386–96, cited in Gillett, 'Why We're More Likely to Remember Content with Images and Video'.
[3] Tania Harris, *The Church Who Hears God's Voice: Equipping Everyone to Recognise and Respond to the Spirit* (Milton Keynes: Paternoster), pp. 80–81; Tanya M. Luhrmann, *When God Talks Back: Understanding the American Evangelical Relationship with God* (New York, NY: Vintage, 2012), p. 195; Danah Zohar and Ian Marshall, *Spiritual Intelligence: The Ultimate Intelligence* (London: Bloomsbury, 2000), pp. 93–5, 107–11.

4. When a Dream Is Not a Dream

[1] For a more comprehensive discussion of the experience of dreams and visions in the early church and beyond, see Morton T. Kelsey, *God, Dreams, and Revelation: A Christian Interpretation of Dreams* (Minneapolis, MN: Augsburg Fortress, rev. edn, 1991), chs 5 and 6.
[2] Quoted in Louis M. Savary, Patricia H. Berne and Strephon Kaplan Williams, *Dreams and Spiritual Growth: A Judeo-Christian Way of Dreamwork* (New York, NY: Paulist Press), p. 41.
[3] Kelsey, *God, Dreams, and Revelation*, p. 139.
[4] Kelsey, *God, Dreams, and Revelation*, p. 142.
[5] Kelsey, *God, Dreams, and Revelation*, p. 143.
[6] For more on revelatory experiences during the Reformation, see Tania Harris, *The Church Who Hears God's Voice: Equipping Everyone to Recognise and Respond to the Spirit* (Milton Keynes: Paternoster), pp. 20–22.

7. With notable exceptions, for example among the Anabaptists, and during the Wesleyan revivals and the Great Awakening in North America.
8. Kelsey, *God, Dreams, and Revelation*, pp. 99–100.
9. John A. Sanford, *Dreams: God's Forgotten Language* (New York, NY: HarperCollins, rev. edn, 1989).
10. Tania M. Harris, 'The Place of Contemporary Revelatory Experiences in Pentecostal Theology', *Journal of the European Pentecostal Theological Association* 41.2 (2021): pp. 93–107; David Hymes, 'Toward an Old Testament Theology of Dreams and Visions from a Pentecostal-Charismatic Perspective', *Australasian Pentecostal Studies* 14 (2012) https://aps-journal.com/index.php/APS/article/view/117 (accessed 21 Dec. 2019).
11. Tania M. Harris, *Hearing God's Voice: Towards a Theology of Contemporary Pentecostal Revelatory Experience* (Leiden: Brill, 2023), p. 158. Examples of this approach: Dallas Willard, *Hearing God: Developing a Conversational Relationship with God* (New York, NY: HarperCollins, 1993), loc. 45–6; Joyce Meyer, *How to Hear from God: Learn to Know His Voice and Make Right Decisions* (New York, NY: Warner, 2003), pp. 45, 48.
12. Harris, *Hearing God's Voice*, pp. 18–20.
13. See Harris, *Hearing God's Voice*, pp. 23–4.
14. Read the full story in my first book, Tania Harris, *God Conversations: Stories of How God Speaks and What Happens When We Listen* (Milton Keynes: Authentic Media, 2017).

5. Where Do Dreams Come From?

1. Quoted in Morton T. Kelsey, *God, Dreams, and Revelation: A Christian Interpretation of Dreams* (Minneapolis, MN: Augsburg Fortress, rev. edn, 1991), p. 177.
2. Kelsey, *God, Dreams, and Revelation*, p. 175.
3. Osman Shabir, 'Why Do We Dream?' *News Medical* (2021) www.news-medical.net/health/Why-Do-We-Dream.aspx (accessed 16 Nov. 2021).
4. Bessel van der Kolk, *The Body Keeps the Score: Brain, Mind, and Body in the Healing of Trauma* (New York, NY: Penguin, 2015), p. 260.
5. Louis M. Savary, Patricia H. Berne and Strephon Kaplan Williams, *Dreams and Spiritual Growth: A Judeo-Christian Way of Dreamwork* (New York, NY: Paulist Press), p. 199.

Notes

6 John A. Sanford, *Dreams: God's Forgotten Language* (New York, NY: HarperCollins, rev. edn, 1989), p. 25.

7 The Global South refers broadly to the regions of Latin America, Asia, Africa and Oceania.

8 Amos Yong, *The Spirit of Creation: Modern Science and Divine Action in the Pentecostal-Charismatic Imagination* (Grand Rapids, MI: Eerdmans, 2011), p. 176.

9 Jon Gathje, 'All the Saints of God: Expanding a Plural Pneumatology through the Communion of the Saints', *Journal of Pentecostal Theology* 25.1 (2016): p. 110.

10 But as Veli-Matti Kärkkäinen emphasizes, this acknowledgement of the presence of the saints who have passed should never move towards ancestor worship: *Christian Theology in the Pluralistic World: A Global Introduction* (Grand Rapids, MI: Eerdmans, 2019), p. 471.

11 Mama Agnes's story is told in her own words in Nicola Neal's book, *Turning Tables: The Transforming Power of an Upside-Down Kingdom* (UK: Mirembe Media, 2023), pp. 65–8.

12 Art Jahnke, 'Unholy Spirits', *Bostonia* (Spring 2009) https://www.bu.edu/bostonia/spring09/nightmares/ (accessed 3 Nov. 2022). See also Patrick McNamara, *Nightmares: The Science and Solution of Those Frightening Visions during Sleep* (Westport, CT: Praeger, 2008).

13 Charles H. Kraft, *I Give You Authority: Practicing the Authority Jesus Gave Us* (Grand Rapids: Chosen, rev. edn, 2012), p. 174. Also Peter Horrobin, *Healing Through Deliverance: The Foundation and Practice of Deliverance Ministry* (Grand Rapids, MI: Chosen, 2008), p. 330.

14 Jahnke, 'Unholy Spirits'.

15 Victor H. Matthews, *Social World of the Hebrew Prophets* (Peabody, MA: Hendrickson, 2001), p. 20.

16 Jean-Marie Husser, *Dreams and Dream Narratives in the Biblical World* (Sheffield: Sheffield Academic Press, 2001), p. 19.

17 Charles H. Kraft, *Deep Wounds, Deep Healing: An Introduction to Deep-Level Healing* (Ventura, CA: Gospel Light, 2010), p. 65.

18 John and Paula Sanford, *Healing the Wounded Spirit* (Tulsa, OK: Victory House, 1985), pp. 298–300; Horrobin, *Healing Through Deliverance*, pp. 330–31.

19 The writings of Charles Kraft, John and Paula Sanford, and Neal Lozano referenced in this book are helpful guides in this area.

20 Neal Lozano, *Unbound: A Practical Guide to Deliverance* (Grand Rapids, MI: Chosen, 2010), p. 41.

[21] Kraft, *I Give You Authority*, p. 175.
[22] 'Nightmares', *Psychology Today* (26 Apr. 2022) https://www.psychologytoday.com/intl/conditions/nightmares (accessed 3 Nov. 2022).
[23] Savary, Berne and Williams, *Dreams and Spiritual Growth*, pp. 160ff.
[24] Savary, Berne and Williams, *Dreams and Spiritual Growth*, pp. 161–3.

7. Peter's Vision of an Unappetizing Lunch

[1] For more on this testing process and its use as a model for discernment in church history, see Tania Harris, *The Church Who Hears God's Voice: Equipping Everyone to Recognise and Respond to the Spirit* (Milton Keynes: Paternoster, 2022), chs 11–12 (pp. 127–50).

8. Your Customized Dream Dictionary

[1] 'Red Cross Symbol Symbolizes Neutrality, Impartiality', *Red Cross* (4 June 2020) https://www.redcross.org/about-us/news-and-events/news/2020/red-cross-emblem-symbolizes-neutrality-impartiality.html (accessed 26 Oct. 2023).
[2] Michael J. Gorman, *Reading Revelation Responsibly: Uncivil Worship and Witness. Following the Lamb into the New Creation* (Eugene, OR: Cascade, 2011), p. 96 (quoting author Hal Lindsey).

10. John's Vision of the Heavenly Government

[1] According to Michael J. Gorman, Revelation made it into the canon by the 'skin of its teeth': *Reading Revelation Responsibly: Uncivil Worship and Witness. Following the Lamb into the New Creation* (Eugene, OR: Cascade, 2011), p. 90.
[2] As Joel Neal points out, it is crucial that Revelation be interpreted with an appreciation for its genre as a prophetic visionary experience: 'John's Visionary Experience as an Interpretive Key to the Book of Revelation', *Journal of Pentecostal Theology* 31 (2022): pp. 40–78.
[3] Popular understandings of Revelation as reflected in books such as the Left Behind series draw on a theology that was invented in the nineteenth century and radically departs from historical understandings, particularly

Notes 225

those of the early church. The key proponent of this teaching, John N. Darby, was a cessationist who didn't believe in Spirit-speaking experiences beyond the Bible.

4 Craig R. Koester includes several examples of strange interpretations of Revelation, including dates for the end of the world: *Revelation and the End of All Things* (Grand Rapids, MI: Eerdmans, 2nd edn, 2018), loc. 342–495.

5 Revelation's author was likely to have been a Jew who knew his Greek Old Testament well. He must also have been significant enough to be considered a threat to authorities. See Gregory Beale and David Campbell, *Revelation: A Shorter Commentary* (Grand Rapids, MI: Eerdmans, 2014), loc. 199.

6 The fact that *seven* churches are named and later used as a common number in the vision series hints at the possibility that the visions may have been intended for the entire region: N.T. Wright, *Revelation for Everyone* (London: SPCK, 2011), p. 8. Also John Christopher Thomas and Frank D. Macchia, *Revelation*, Two Horizons New Testament Commentary (Grand Rapids, MI: Eerdmans, 2016), loc. 709.

7 Thomas and Macchia, *Revelation*, loc. 693.

8 For a helpful description of Rome's policy of violence, see Tom Holland, *Dominion: The Making of the Western Mind* (London: Little, Brown, 2019), p. 90.

9 For a description of the ways emperors were viewed in this era, see Jeremy Duncan, *Upside-Down Apocalypse: Grounding Revelation in the Gospel of Peace* (Harrisonburg, VA: Herald Press, 2022), pp. 74–8.

10 Gorman, *Reading Revelation Responsibly*, p. 63. These titles were used by Statius in his writings about Domitian.

11 Holland, *Dominion*, p. 100. Also 'Lord of All', God, Son of God and 'Saviour': Gorman, *Reading Revelation Responsibly*, p. 64.

12 The dating of Revelation is notoriously difficult. Arguments have been made for three options: 1. After the fall of Jerusalem in 70 CE during the reign of Emperor Domitian (81–96 CE) (the view held for the first eighteen centuries). 2. Before the fall of Jerusalem at the time of Emperor Nero (64–70 CE). 3. A combination of the first two; i.e. the vision was experienced during the time of Nero but written down during Domitian's reign: Thomas and Macchia, *Revelation*, loc. 855. While there is no consensus on Revelation's dating, the first-century hearers of the visions would either have known of the events in the past or have been aware of the tension between the Jews and the Romans that would go on to precipitate those events.

13 Wright explores this dimension of persecution in the church of Smyrna where there was a lively synagogue: *Revelation for Everyone*, p. 17 (see Rev. 2:9; 3:9).

[14] Adela Yarbro Collins notes five elements of personal and communal trauma that involved the Romans as adversaries of Christians. These included persecutions under Nero, the destruction of Jerusalem, the polytheistic imperial religious cult, martyrdom and the deportation of John. Quoted in Denny J. Weaver, *The Nonviolent Atonement* (Grand Rapids, MI: Eerdmans, 2nd edn, 2011), loc. 399.

[15] This imagery is more explicitly found in the Apocrypha (2 Esdras 11 and 12): Wright, *Revelation for Everyone*, p. 53.

[16] Beale estimates over 500 allusions to Old Testament imagery – more than all other New Testament books combined: Beale and Campbell, *Revelation*, loc. 180, 492.

[17] Gorman, *Reading Revelation Responsibly*, p. 143.

[18] Duncan, *Upside-Down Apocalypse*, p. 76, quoting Dio Cassius, *Roman History* 67.4.3.

[19] Duncan, *Upside-Down Apocalypse*, p. 75.

[20] Significantly, Jesus had spoken about the disciples sitting on twelve thrones, although as he explained, his idea of power and rule was vastly different from theirs (Luke 22:29–30).

[21] Wright, *Revelation for Everyone*, p. 44; Gorman, *Reading Revelation Responsibly*, p. 145. Another option is that the twenty-four elders are angelic beings: Richard Bauckham, *The Theology of the Book of Revelation* (Cambridge: Cambridge University Press, 1993), p. 33.

[22] Wright, *Revelation for Everyone*, p. 47; Gorman, *Reading Revelation Responsibly*, p. 145.

[23] Duncan, *Upside-Down Apocalypse*, p. 79.

[24] Duncan, *Upside-Down Apocalypse*, p. 79.

11. More on Symbols (1): The Dragon and a Pregnant Woman

[1] The most significant difference between the trumpets and the bowls is the *scope*; for example, *all* sea creatures die when the fourth bowl is poured out (Rev. 16:3), not just one-third, as was the case with the sounding of the second trumpet (Rev. 8:9): Michael J. Gorman, *Reading Revelation Responsibly: Uncivil Worship and Witness. Following the Lamb into the New Creation* (Eugene, OR: Cascade, 2011), p. 189.

[2] Gorman, *Reading Revelation Responsibly*, p. 186.

3 Denny J. Weaver takes this approach in *The Nonviolent Atonement* (Grand Rapids, MI: Eerdmans, 2nd edn, 2011), loc. 357–91.
4 Weaver, *The Nonviolent Atonement*, loc. 365.
5 Weaver, *The Nonviolent Atonement*, loc. 370. Furthermore, the deaths by sword, famine, pestilence and wild animals in seal four could have harked back to Nero's devastating reign in 54–68 CE when Christians were first martyred and when the empire endured a bubonic plague that claimed 30,000 people in one season. And the earth-shattering events of seal six could easily align with the attack on the temple and the city of Jerusalem under Vespasian: Weaver, *The Nonviolent Atonement*, loc. 391.
6 This understanding of the seals, trumpets and bowls as repetitive symbols is widely held. See N.T. Wright, *Revelation for Everyone* (London: SPCK, 2011), p. 63; Gorman, *Reading Revelation Responsibly*, p. 82; Beale and Campbell, *Revelation*, loc. 586–617.
7 Compare with the righteous people who are sealed in Ezek. 9: Wright, *Revelation for Everyone*, p. 70.
8 Most scholars believe that the 144,000 and the countless multitude represent the same group, i.e. the people of God: Wright, *Revelation for Everyone*, p. 70.
9 Weaver, *The Nonviolent Atonement*, loc. 336–8; Richard Bauckham, *The Theology of Revelation* (Cambridge: Cambridge University Press, 1993), p. 137; Gorman, *Reading Revelation Responsibly*, pp. 177–8; Wright, *Revelation for Everyone*, pp. 70, 74.
10 Duncan, *Upside-Down Apocalypse*, pp. 130–3.
11 Weaver, *The Nonviolent Atonement*, loc. 417–22; Gorman, *Reading Revelation Responsibly*, p. 175; Wright, *Revelation for Everyone*, p. 107.
12 Duncan, *Upside-Down Apocalypse*, p. 130.

12. More on Symbols (2): Two Kingdoms at War

1 This characterization is made more explicit with a reference to seven kings in subsequent visions (Rev. 17:9–11).
2 Daniel's visions pointed to the promise of a Messiah who would overcome all human empires and restore God's reign to the world (with the *little horn* rising up against the larger horn). Of course, his vision was fulfilled with Jesus' coming, but not in a way anyone expected.
3 Jeremy Duncan, *Upside-Down Apocalypse: Grounding Revelation in the Gospel of Peace* (Harrisonburg, VA: Herald Press, 2022), p. 143.

[4] Though monstrous creatures can also represent the demonic.

[5] The sea-beast probably represents the emperor himself, having come from the west by way of the Aegean Sea. The land-beast likely symbolizes the local governors, religious officials and merchants who promoted Rome's strategies among the people: Michael J. Gorman, *Reading Revelation Responsibly: Uncivil Worship and Witness. Following the Lamb into the New Creation* (Eugene, OR: Cascade, 2011), p. 167. Also Richard Bauckham, *The Theology of Revelation* (Cambridge: Cambridge University Press, 1993), p. 88.

[6] While we can't be sure that this was a direct requirement at the time of John's visions, it is significant that at the turn of the first century there is evidence of Christians being tested for their allegiance to Rome by the requirement to either curse Christ, burn incense to an image of Caesar or make a sacrifice to the Greco-Roman gods: Jon K. Newton, *A Pentecostal Commentary on Revelation* (Eugene, OR: Wipf & Stock, 2021), p. 18.

[7] The drunken courtesan may also be likened to the goddess Roma, who was often depicted on coins sitting on the seven hills of Rome: Duncan, *Upside-Down Apocalypse*, p. 150.

[8] Gorman, *Reading Revelation Responsibly*, p. 65.

[9] Katie A. Haldane, 'Christ as Ascended God-Emperor: Visualising Apotheosis in Revelation 19:11–16', unpublished article.

[10] In the ancient world, cities were commonly personified as women: Bauckham, *The Theology of Revelation*, pp. 126ff.

13. How Do You Know It's a God-Dream?

[1] Augustine himself warned that the book should only be included in the canon 'with an admonition against using the book speculatively' (*City of God*, 20.6–9).

[2] Based on *The Passion of Saints Perpetua and Felicity in St. Gallen*, Stiftsbibliothek, Cod. Sang. 577 (ninth/tenth centuries).

[3] Alan Kreider, *The Patient Ferment of the Early Church: The Improbable Rise of Christianity in the Roman Empire* (Grand Rapids, MI: Baker Academic, 2016), pp. 45–8.

14. After We Wake Up

[1] Morton T. Kelsey, *God, Dreams, and Revelation: A Christian Interpretation of Dreams* (Minneapolis, MN: Augsburg Fortress, rev. edn, 1991), p. 81.

[2] For more on the lasting impact of the growing Christian church on western values, read Tom Holland, *Dominion: The Making of the Western Mind* (London: Little, Brown, 2019); John Dickson, *Humilitas: A Lost Key to Life, Love and Leadership* (Grand Rapids, MI: Zondervan, 2011); and Iain Provan, *Seriously Dangerous Religion: What the Old Testament Really Says and Why It Matters* (Waco, TX: Baylor University Press, 2014).

15. Meeting God in a Dream

[1] Not his real name.
[2] Nicola Menzie, 'Report: ISIS Fighter Who "Enjoyed" Killing Christians Wants to Follow Jesus after Dreaming of Man in White Who Told Him "You Are Killing My People"', *The Christian Post* (3 June 2015) https://www.christianpost.com/news/report-isis-fighter-who-enjoyed-killing-christians-wants-to-follow-jesus-after-dreaming-of-man-in-white-who-told-him-you-are-killing-my-people.html (accessed 1 Sept. 2022).
[3] Her story is retold in Tania Harris, *The Church Who Hears God's Voice: Equipping Everyone to Recognise and Respond to the Spirit* (Milton Keynes: Paternoster, 2022), and is originally recorded in Tom Doyle and Gregory Webster, *Dreams and Visions: Is Jesus Awakening the Muslim World?* (Nashville, TN: Thomas Nelson, 2012).
[4] Tom Doyle, *Breakthrough: The Return of Hope to the Middle East* (Downers Grove, IL: IVP, 2009). Since the publication of this book, missionaries estimate the figure to be more like 50%.
[5] We see this scenario in the case of Daniel, where his 'interpretation' of King Nebuchadnezzar's dream was actually a separate revelation since he didn't even know the dream's content! (Dan. 2). Like Daniel, we may receive an interpretation supernaturally on behalf of another person, rather than working through the five-step framework. This interpretation should be delivered with humility and grace, always allowing the recipient to test and discern the meaning of the dream for themselves.

16. Awakening Your Dreams

[1] R.K. Gnuse, *The Dream Theophany of Samuel: Its Structure in Relation to Ancient Near Eastern Dreams and Its Theological Significance* (New York, NY: University Press of America, 1984), p. 58.

Bibliography

Aune, David E. *Prophecy in Early Christianity and the Ancient Mediterranean World* (Grand Rapids, MI: Eerdmans, 1983).

Bar, Shaul. *A Letter That Has Not been Read: Dreams in the Hebrew Bible* (Cincinnati, OH: Hebrew Union College Press, 2001).

Bauckham, Richard. *The Theology of the Book of Revelation* (Cambridge: Cambridge University Press, 1993) (Kindle edition).

———. *The Climax of Prophecy: Studies on the Book of Revelation* (Edinburgh: T&T Clark, 1993).

Beale, Gregory, and David Campbell. *Revelation: A Shorter Commentary* (Grand Rapids, MI: Eerdmans, 2014) (Kindle edition).

Bulkeley, Kelly. *Dreaming in the World's Religions: A Comparative History* (New York, NY: New York University Press, 2008).

Cerf-Ducastel, Barbara, and Claire Murphy, 'Neural Substrates of Cross-modal Olfactory Recognition Memory: An fMRI study', *Neuroimage* 31.1 (2006): pp. 386–96.

Charsley, Simon. 'Dreams in African Churches.' pp 153–76 in *Dreaming, Religion, and Society in Africa* (ed. M.C. Jedrej and Rosalind Shaw; Leiden: Brill, 1992).

Cottier, Cody. 'Do Animals Dream and How Can We Tell?' *Discover* (9 September 2023) https://www.discovermagazine.com/planet-earth/do-animals-dream-and-how-can-we-tell (accessed 8 Sept. 2023).

DeSilva, David. *Unholy Allegiances: Heeding Revelation's Warning* (Peabody, MA: Hendrickson, 2013).

Dickson, John. *Humilitas: A Lost Key to Life, Love and Leadership* (Grand Rapids, MI: Zondervan, 2011).

Doyle, Tom, *Breakthrough: The Return of Hope to the Middle East* (Downers Grove, IL: IVP, 2009).

Doyle, Tom, and Greg Webster. *Dreams and Visions: Is Jesus Awakening the Muslim World?* (Nashville, TN: Thomas Nelson, 2012).

Droll, Anna M. *Dreams and Visions in African Pentecostal Spirituality* (Leiden: Brill, 2024).

Duncan, Jeremy. *Upside-Down Apocalypse: Grounding Revelation in the Gospel of Peace* (Harrisonburg, VA: Herald Press, 2022) (Kindle edition).

Eliade, Mircea. *Myths, Dreams and Mysteries* (New York, NY: Harper & Brothers, 1960).

Freud, Sigmund. *A General Introduction to Psychoanalysis* (New York, NY: Washington Square Press, 1960).

———. *The Interpretation of Dreams* (New York, NY: Basic, 1995).

Gathje, Jon. 'All the Saints of God: Expanding a Plural Pneumatology through the Communion of the Saints'. *Journal of Pentecostal Theology* 25.1 (2016): pp. 107–22.

Gillett, Rachel. 'Why We're More Likely to Remember Content with Images and Video'. *Fast Company* (18 September 2014) https://www.fastcompany.com/3035856/why-were-more-likely-to-remember-content-with-images-and-video-infogr (accessed 12 Nov. 2020).

Gnuse, R.K. *The Dream Theophany of Samuel: Its Structure in Relation to Ancient Near Eastern Dreams and Its Theological Significance* (New York, NY: University Press of America, 1984).

Gorman, Michael J. *Reading Revelation Responsibly: Uncivil Worship and Witness. Following the Lamb into the New Creation* (Eugene, OR: Cascade, 2011) (Kindle edition).

Haldane, Katie A. 'Christ as Ascended God-Emperor: Visualising Apotheosis in Revelation 19:11–16', unpublished article.

Harris, Tania M. *The Church Who Hears God's Voice* (Milton Keynes: Paternoster, 2022).

———. *God Conversations: Stories of How God Speaks and What Happens When We Listen* (Milton Keynes: Authentic Media, 2017).

———. *Hearing God's Voice: Towards a Theology of Contemporary Pentecostal Revelatory Experience* (Leiden: Brill, 2023).

———. 'The Place of Contemporary Revelatory Experiences in Pentecostal Theology'. *Journal of the European Pentecostal Theological Association* 41.2 (2021): pp. 93–107.

Holland, Tom. *Dominion: The Making of the Western Mind* (London: Little, Brown, 2019) (Kindle edition).

Horrobin, Peter. *Healing Through Deliverance: The Foundation and Practice of Deliverance Ministry* (Grand Rapids, MI: Chosen, 2008).

Hospice & Palliative Care, Buffalo, 'Study Conducted by The Palliative Care Institute Indicates Dreams and Visions Provide a Profound Source of Meaning and Comfort for the Dying' (3 April 2022) https://www.hospicebuffalo.com/news/press-releases/study-conducted-palliative-care-institute-indicates-dreams-and-visions-provide-profound-source-meaning-and-comfort-dying (accessed 14 March 2024).

Husser, Jean-Marie. *Dreams and Dream Narratives in the Biblical World* (Sheffield: Sheffield Academic Press, 2001).

Hymes, David. 'Toward an Old Testament Theology of Dreams and Visions from a Pentecostal-Charismatic Perspective'. *Australasian Pentecostal Studies* 14 (2012) https://aps-journal.com/index.php/APS/article/view/117 (accessed 21 Dec. 2019).

Jahnke, Art. 'Unholy Spirits'. *Bostonia* (Spring 2009) https://www.bu.edu/bostonia/spring09/nightmares (accessed 3 Nov. 2022).

Jung, C.G. *Collected Works, vol. 5: Symbols of Transformation* (New York, NY: Random House/Pantheon, 1956).

Kärkkäinen, Veli-Matti. *Christian Theology in the Pluralistic World: A Global Introduction* (Grand Rapids, MI: Eerdmans, 2019).

Kelsey, Morton T. *God, Dreams, and Revelation: A Christian Interpretation of Dreams* (Minneapolis, MN: Augsburg Fortress, rev. edn, 1991).

Koester, Craig R. *Revelation and the End of All Things* (Grand Rapids, MI: Eerdmans, 2nd edn, 2018) (Kindle edition).

Kraft, Charles H. *Deep Wounds, Deep Healing: An Introduction to Deep-Level Healing* (Ventura, CA: Gospel Light, 2010).

———. *I Give You Authority: Practicing the Authority Jesus Gave Us* (Grand Rapids, MI: Chosen, rev. edn, 2012).

Kreider, Alan. *The Patient Ferment of the Early Church: The Improbable Rise of Christianity in the Roman Empire* (Grand Rapids, MI: Baker Academic, 2016).

LaMotte, Sandee. 'Our Dreams Are Changing as We Emerge from the Pandemic. Here's How', *CNN* (14 July 2023) https://edition.cnn.com/2021/07/12/health/dreams-pandemic-opening-wellness/index.html (accessed 14 Sept. 2021).

Lindblom, Johannes. *Prophecy in Ancient Israel* (Philadelphia, PA: Fortress, 1962).

Lozano, Neal. *Unbound: A Practical Guide to Deliverance* (Grand Rapids, MI: Chosen, 2010).

Luhrmann, Tanya M. *When God Talks Back: Understanding the American Evangelical Relationship with God* (New York, NY: Vintage, 2012).

Matthews, Victor H. *Social World of the Hebrew Prophets* (Peabody, MA: Hendrickson, 2001).

McNamara, Patrick. *Nightmares: The Science and Solution of Those Frightening Visions during Sleep* (Westport, CT: Praeger, 2008).

Menzie, Nicola. 'Report: ISIS Fighter Who "Enjoyed" Killing Christians Wants to Follow Jesus after Dreaming of Man in White Who Told Him "You Are Killing My People"'. *The Christian Post* (3 June 2015) https://www.christianpost.com/news/report-isis-fighter-who-enjoyed-killing-christians-wants-to-follow-jesus-after-dreaming-of-man-in-white-who-told-him-you-are-killing-my-people.html (accessed 1 Sept. 2022).

Meyer, Joyce. *How to Hear from God: Learn to Know His Voice and Make Right Decisions* (New York, NY: Warner, 2003).

Miller, John B. F. *Convinced That God Had Called Us: Dreams, Visions and the Perception of God's Will in Luke-Acts* (Leiden/Boston: Brill, 2007).

Neal, Joel. 'John's Visionary Experience as an Interpretive Key to the Book of Revelation'. *Journal of Pentecostal Theology* 31 (2022): pp. 40–78.

Neal, Nicola. *Turning Tables: The Transforming Power of an Upside-Down Kingdom* (UK: Mirembe Media, 2023).

Newton, Jon K. *A Pentecostal Commentary on Revelation* (Eugene, OR: Wipf & Stock, 2021) (Kindle edition).

Niditch, S. *The Symbolic Vision in Biblical Tradition* (Chico, CA: Scholars Press, 1980).

Nielsen, Tore, and Russell A. Powell. 'Dreams of the Rarebit Fiend: Food and Diet as Instigators of Bizarre and Disturbing Dreams'. *Frontiers in Psychology* 6 (2015) https://www.academia.edu/10605094/Dreams_of_the_Rarebit_Fiend_food_and_diet_as_instigators_of_bizarre_and_disturbing_dreams_2015_ (accessed 14 March 2024).

'Nightmares', *Psychology Today* (26 April 2022) https://www.psychologytoday.com/intl/conditions/nightmares (accessed 3 November 2022).

Oppenheim, A. Leo. *The Interpretation of Dreams in the Ancient Near East, with a Translation of an Assyrian Dream Book* (Whitefish, MT: Literary Licensing, LLC, 2011).

Paunovich, Zoran. *In Your Dreams* (O'Halloran Hill, South Australia: Golden Grain, 2003).

Provan, Iain. *Seriously Dangerous Religion: What the Old Testament Really Says and Why It Matters* (Waco, TX: Baylor University Press, 2014).

'Red Cross Symbol Symbolizes Neutrality, Impartiality', *Red Cross* (4 June 2020) https://www.redcross.org/about-us/news-and-events/news/2020/red-cross-emblem-symbolizes-neutrality-impartiality.html (accessed 26 Oct. 2023).

Sandford, John Loren. *Elijah Among Us: Understanding and Responding to God's Prophets Today* (Grand Rapids, MI: Chosen, 2002).

Sandford, John, and Paula Sandford. *Healing the Wounded Spirit* (Tulsa, OK: Victory House, 1985).

Sanford, John A. *Dreams: God's Forgotten Language* (New York, NY: HarperCollins, rev. edn, 1989).

Savary, Louis M., Patricia H. Berne and Strephon Kaplan Williams. *Dreams and Spiritual Growth: A Judeo-Christian Way of Dreamwork* (New York, NY: Paulist Press, 1984).

Shabir, Osman, 'Why Do We Dream?' *News Medical* (2021) www.news-medical.net/health/Why-Do-We-Dream.aspx (accessed 16 Nov. 2021).

Stronstad, Roger. *The Prophethood of All Believers: A Study in Luke's Charismatic Theology*. Journal of Pentecostal Theology Supplement 16 (Sheffield: Sheffield Academic Press, 1999).

Stroumsa, Guy G. 'Dreams and Visions in Early Christian Discourse.' Pages 189–212 in *Dream Cultures: Explorations in the Comparative History of Dreaming* (ed. David D. Shulman and Guy G. Stroumsa; New York, NY: Oxford University Press, 1999).

Tanner, Wilda B. *The Mystical, Magical, Marvelous World of Dreams* (Tahlequah, OK: Sparrow Hawk Press, 1988).

Thomas, John Christopher, and Frank D. Macchia. *Revelation*. Two Horizons New Testament Commentary (Grand Rapids, MI: Eerdmans, 2016) (Kindle edition).

Turner, Max. *The Holy Spirit and Spiritual Gifts: In the New Testament Church and Today* (Grand Rapids, MI: Baker Academic, rev. edn, 2012).

Ullman, Montague, and Stanley Krippner. *Dream Telepathy* (New York, NY: Macmillan, 1973).

Van der Kolk, Bessel. *The Body Keeps the Score: Brain, Mind, and Body in the Healing of Trauma* (New York, NY: Penguin, 2015).

Van der Linden, Sander. 'The Science behind Dreaming'. *Scientific American* (26 July 2011) https://www.scientificamerican.com/article/the-science-behind-dreaming (accessed 8 Nov. 2023).

Weaver, Denny J. *The Nonviolent Atonement* (Grand Rapids, MI: Eerdmans, 2nd edn, 2011).

Willard, Dallas. *Hearing God: Developing a Conversational Relationship with God* (New York, NY: HarperCollins, 1993) (Kindle edition).

Witherington III, Ben. *Jesus the Seer: The Progress of Prophecy* (Peabody, MA: Hendrickson, 1999).

Wright, N.T. *Revelation for Everyone* (London: SPCK, 2011) (Kindle edition).

Yong, Amos. *The Spirit of Creation: Modern Science and Divine Action in the Pentecostal-Charismatic Imagination* (Grand Rapids, MI: Eerdmans, 2011).

Zohar, Danah, and Ian Marshall. *Spiritual Intelligence: The Ultimate Intelligence* (London: Bloomsbury, 2000).

THE COURSE

You've read the book, now join with others in our globally renowned online course!*

The **God Dreams Online Course** includes 7 streamable teaching videos, downloadable Study Guide, discussion questions and practical activities that will equip you to recognise and respond to God's voice in dreams and visions. Hosted by Revd Dr Tania Harris, the course will reinforce the biblical basis for hearing God in dream-visions, help develop your interpretative skills and provide practical opportunities to apply the God-Dreams framework. Continue to grow in your ability to hear the voice of Holy Spirit in the language of pictures. It was never meant to be a one-way conversation!

"…this is what was spoken by the prophet Joel: 'In the last days, God says, I will pour out my Spirit on all people. Your sons and daughters will prophesy, your young men will see visions, your old men will dream dreams.'" (Acts 2:16,17)

godconversations.com/goddreams

*Can also be completed individually.

God Conversations

Stories of how God speaks and what happens when we listen

Tania Harris

Stories of God talking to his people abound throughout the Bible, but we usually only get the highlights. We read: 'God said "Go to Egypt,"' and then, 'Mary and Joseph left for Egypt.' We're not told how God spoke, how they knew it was him, or how they decided to act on what they'd heard.

In *God Conversations*, international speaker and pastor Tania Harris shares insights from her own story of learning to hear God's voice. You'll get to eavesdrop on some contemporary conversations with God in the light of his communication with the ancients. Part memoir, part teaching, this unique and creative collection will help you to recognise God's voice when he speaks and what happens when you do.

978-1-78078-188-4

The Church Who Hears God's Voice

*Equipping everyone to recognise
and respond to the Spirit*

Revd Dr Tania Harris

As the central feature of the Spirit's outpouring at Pentecost and the grand prize of the New Covenant, the prospect of universal access to the Spirit is a powerful but pastorally risky concept. History tells the terrible tales of abuses associated with the claim 'God told me'.

Drawing on insights from theology, history and her groundbreaking PhD research, Harris skilfully presents a comprehensive theology and pastoral strategy for how people in the church, whatever the tradition, can hear the Spirit's voice for themselves.

978-1-78893-246-2

Life, Interrupted

Embracing God's invitations to change

Andrew Stewart-Darling

How many interruptions have you had today? How did you react to them?

Interruptions will always turn up to challenge us. Some will be welcome while others will rock our world. But what if these interruptions are in fact opportunities, holy disruptions even, that God can use to enable us to make significant changes in our lives?

Combining personal stories with biblical teaching and prayers, Andrew Stewart-Darling encourages us to see interruptions as an invitation from God to draw us closer to him.

Become more alert to nudges from the Holy Spirit and be better prepared for life's next curveball.

978-1-78893-344-5

Authentic

We trust you enjoyed reading this book from Authentic. If you want to be informed of any new titles from this author and other releases you can sign up to the Authentic newsletter by scanning below:

Online:
authenticmedia.co.uk

Follow us: